Basic Christian Living

BASIC CHRISTIAN LIVING

A Survey Course on Practical Christianity

DOUGLAS WILSON

canonpress
Moscow, Idaho

Published by Canon Press
P. O. Box 8729, Moscow, ID 83843
800–488–2034 | www.canonpress.com

Douglas Wilson, *Basic Christian Living: A Survey Course on Practical Christianity*
Copyright © 2015 by Douglas Wilson.

Unless otherwise noted, all Scripture references are taken from the Authorized Version.

Cover design by Rachel Rosales.
Interior design by Jessica Evans.

Printed in the United States of America.

Library of Congress Cataloging-in-Publication Data
Wilson, Douglas, 1953-
  Basic Christian living : a survey course on practical Christianity / Douglas Wilson.
     pages cm
  ISBN 978-1-59128-137-5
  1. Theology, Doctrinal--Popular works. 2. Theology, Doctrinal--Textbooks. 3. Christian life--Textbooks. I. Title.
  BT77.W725 2013
  230--dc23

                                        2013010452

15 16 17 18 19 20   10 9 8 7 6 5 4 3 2 1

TABLE OF CONTENTS

THE NATURE OF WORSHIP

Worship and praise are not the same thing. Worship is the foundation for praise, just as it is the foundation for everything else. God has created man to worship Him, and to worship Him rightly.

So what is worship? The biblical answer is that it is glad service. When you offer yourself to God, body and soul, that is worship. The main word in the Old Testament (*aboda*) and in the New (*latreia*) both originally refer to the *service* of slaves or hired servants. So a worship *service* is where you offer yourself—body, soul, and spirit—to God for His work that He has assigned for you.

1. Look up Isaiah 6:1–8, and read through it carefully. If worship is presenting yourself to God for service, and not simply being awestruck at His glory, where does the worship in this passage occur? How is the idea of worship communicated?

_____

_____

2. Now look up Deuteronomy 6:13 and compare it to Matthew 4:10. The command is to worship the Lord your God and serve Him only. Satan wanted Christ's worship (i.e., service). In these passages, when we make ourselves available to God for His service, what instruments of mine am I presenting to Him?

_____

_____

3. Now in Romans 12:1–2, worship is the offering up of the physical body as a living sacrifice. What will the consequence of such worship be on the attitudes of the ones offering it (v. 3)?

_____

_____

4. Romans 6:19 presents another angle on worship. What is offered there, and as what?

_____

_____

5. Having done all this, praise is certainly appropriate. According to Psalm 33:1, for whom is praise appropriate?

_____

_____

6. Undergirded by faithful worship, when is praise appropriate? According to Psalm 34:1 and Hebrews 13:15, when should we praise the Lord?

_____

_____

7. What should we conclude about when we should be worshiping the Lord?

_____

_____

Many of the problems confronting modern Christians is that they diligently try to do the right thing . . . in the wrong categories. They try guitar fingering on a mandolin; they try chess rules on a backgammon board; they apply the rules of French grammar to English. And for us to draw attention to such mistakes is *not* to object to any of these things in particular—chess, guitar, backgammon, whatever. But this is the mistake we make whenever we try to "make a difference" and our activity does not proceed *directly* from a vision of the Almighty Lord, high and lifted up.

[1]The LORD reigneth; let the earth rejoice; let the multitude of isles be glad thereof. [2]Clouds and darkness are round about him: righteousness and judgment are the habitation of his throne. [3]A fire goeth before him, and burneth up his enemies round about. [4]His lightnings enlightened the world: the earth saw, and trembled. [5]The hills melted like wax at the presence of the LORD, at the presence of the Lord of the whole earth. [6]The heavens declare his righteousness, and all the people see his glory. [7]Confounded be all they that serve graven images, that boast themselves of idols: worship him, all ye gods. [8]Zion heard, and was glad; and the daughters of Judah rejoiced because of thy judgments, O LORD. [9]For thou, LORD, art high above all the

earth: thou art exalted far above all gods. [10]Ye that love the LORD, hate evil: he preserveth the souls of his saints; he delivereth them out of the hand of the wicked. [11]Light is sown for the righteous, and gladness for the upright in heart. [12]Rejoice in the LORD, ye righteous; and give thanks at the remembrance of his holiness." (Ps. 97:1–12)

8. God *reigns*, and what is called to rejoice (v. 1)?

_____

9. His holiness is not what we might assume—His righteousness and judgment are compared to what (v. 2)?

_____

10. A fire precedes Him, and so what happens to His enemies (v. 3)?

_____

11. Lightning flashes, and the whole created order sees it, and what is the response (v. 4)?

_____

12. In the presence of God, hills and mountains melt in what way (v. 5)?

_____

13. The heavens preach, and what does everyone sees as a result (v. 6)?

_____

14. A curse is pronounced—confounded be all false worshipers. And what are all the gods summoned to do (v. 7)?

_____

15. When this is proclaimed, Zion hears and is glad. What do the daughters of Judah do (v. 8)?

_____

16. Why do we rejoice (v. 9)?

_____

17. This transcendent sense of true worship has potent ethical ramifications—what are those who love the Lord called to hate (v. 10)?

_____

18. In this setting, there are those who return the hatred. What does God do (v. 10)?

_____

19. Light is sown for the righteous. Who receives gladness (v. 11)?

_____

20. We are summoned by God to therefore rejoice. What are we to do as we remember His holiness (v. 12)?

_____

Holiness is not manageable (v. 2). Holiness does not come in a shrink-wrapped box. Holiness is not *marketable*. Holiness is not tame. Holiness is not sweetsy-nice. Holiness is not represented by kitschy figurines. Holiness is not smarmy. Holiness is not unctuous. Holiness is not domesticated. But if you worship a god who is housebroken to all your specifications, what is the result? Depression, and a regular need for sedatives—better living through chemistry.

Holiness is wild. Holiness is three tornadoes in a row. Holiness is a series of black thunderheads coming in off the bay. Holiness is impolite. Holiness is darkness to make a sinful man tremble. Holiness beckons us to that darkness, where we do not meet ghouls and ghosts, but rather the righteousness of God. Holiness is a consuming fire. Holiness melts the world. And when we fear and worship a God like this, what is the result? Gladness of heart.

Worship a god who does nothing but kittens and pussy willows and you will end in despair. Worship the God of the jagged edge, the God whose holiness *cannot* be made palatable for the middle-class American consumer, and the result is deep *gladness*. Do you hear that? Gladness, *not* pomposity. And, thank God, such gladness does not make us parade about with cheeks puffed slighted out, or speak with lots of rotund vowels, or strut with a sanctimonious air. Gladness, laughter, joy—set *these* before you. This is deep Christian faith, and not what so many are marketing today in the name of Jesus. The tragedy is that in the name of relevance the current expression of the faith today is superficial *all the way down*.

Those who love and worship the Lord are called to hate evil. So this is why an ethical application of the vision of the holy is most necessary. If we bypass this vision of who God actually is, the necessary result will be a prissy moralism, and not the robust morality of the

Christian faith. The distance between moralism and true morality is vast, and the thing that creates this distance is *knowledge of the holy*. Those who content themselves with petty rules spend all their time fussing about with hemlines, curfews, and scruples about alcohol. But those who see this folly and go off in their own little libertine direction are no better. The former act as though their moralism is grounded on the dictates of a gremlin-like god who lives in their attic, but his word is *law*. The latter say that this is stupid, and aspire to become the gremlin themselves. There are two parts: love the Lord, hate evil.

According to this psalm, how should we define right worship? The answer is that *right worship* occurs when the congregation of God approaches Him, *sees Him as He is*, and responds rightly, as He has commanded—in joy and glad submission. Such worship necessitates turning away from all idols (v. 7), and turning to the holy God who *cannot* be manipulated. And in this psalm alone, what does right worship do? What effect does it have? What are the results? The earth rejoices (v. 1). All the islands are glad (v. 1). His enemies are consumed with the fire that goes before Him (v. 3). The earth is illuminated by His lightning, and trembles (v. 4). In the presence of the Lord (and in worship we *are* in the presence of the Lord), the hills melt (v. 5). The heavens preach, and the people see His glory (v. 6). Idolaters are flummoxed, confounded (v. 7). The universal call to worship is even issued to the idols (v. 7). Zion hears and is *glad*, and the daughters of Judah *rejoice* (v. 8). The name of God is exalted above every name (v. 9). The saints of God learn to hate evil, and God preserves them from those who persecute them (v. 10). Light and gladness are sown in our hearts (v. 11). His righteous people rejoice, and are grateful when they remember His holiness (v. 12).

21. Describe in a few words the difference between praise and worship.

_____

_____

_____

_____

_____

_____

_____

_____

22. Describe the relation between a perception of God's holiness and the right kind of worship.

_____

_____

_____

_____

_____

_____

_____

Those who *serve* graven images are confounded (v. 7). Those who worship false gods cannot be anything but confounded. Those who worship the true God falsely are missing the scriptural call as well. But those who worship rightly will inherit the earth.

FORGIVENESS OF SIN

The Lord Jesus was born into a *sinful* world. His advent was not designed as an inspirational moment to crown all the others, but rather He was sent as a *Savior*. He came to bring forgiveness, and consequently if there is anything His followers should understand, receive, and practice, it is forgiveness.

1. Look up Matthew 1:19–21, a passage which records the dream that Joseph received. Why was Jesus named *Jesus*? What was the point?

_____

_____

2. Now look up Hebrews 10:16–18. There are two main characteristics of the new covenant that are mentioned there. What are they?

_____

_____

Now after Joseph discovered that Mary was pregnant (and he knew that *he* wasn't the father), the only reasonable conclusion for him to draw was that Mary had been unfaithful to him (Mt. 1:19). But he did not want to humiliate her, so he resolved to divorce her quietly. While he was deciding what to do, an angel appeared to him in a dream, called him a son of David, and told him that Mary had conceived as result of the work of the Holy Spirit (v. 20). The angel told him, further, that the baby would be a boy and that Joseph was to name Him *Jesus*. The reason for the name is that He would save His people from their sins (v. 21). The name *Jesus* is the New Testament equivalent of *Joshua*, which means that "God is salvation," a meaning that Matthew confirms, adding the important detail that the salvation is from sin.

Jeremiah had looked forward to the coming of the new covenant—a time when Israel and Judah would be transformed into faithful covenant-keepers. In the eighth chapter of Hebrews, the entire passage from Jeremiah is quoted. In Hebrews 10, it is quoted again in abridged form, emphasizing the key details of the new covenant. These key terms were the internalization of the law (Heb. 10:16), and the forgiveness of sins (v. 16). And where there is remission, there is no further need for sin offerings (v. 17).

3. So again, what does the name *Jesus* mean?

_____

4. What does the new covenant promise us?

_____

God offers sinful human beings deep forgiveness. The Lord Jesus did not come, live a perfect life, die on the cross, and come back from the dead in order to dab around the edges of our wound. Our complicity in the sin of Adam, and our continuing screwed-up-ness required a great remedy, which could not be had apart from the work of a great Savior.

5. So look up Matthew 9:12. Who did Jesus come for?

_____

_____

6. If Jesus came for messed-up people, then can you disqualify yourself from His grace by being all messed up?

_____

_____

But remember that Jesus is saving us from our sins, and not merely from the consequences of our sins—from sin itself and not just from condemnation for sin. And one of the central sins He is saving us from is the sin of the double standard—wanting to receive forgiveness on easy terms, and wanting to extend it with the heart of a stickler for justice. We want to borrow easily, and lend with difficulty. We want our fingers open to receive, and have our fist clenched for giving.

But Jesus has given us fair warning about how we do not receive forgiveness on our terms. Not at all. In the Lord's Prayer, we are taught to say this to *God*—"And forgive us our debts, as we forgive our debtors" (Mt. 6:12). "Dear God, please harbor toward me all the thoughts I harbor toward others." Do the words stick in the throat? "This is how my heavenly Father will treat each of you unless you forgive your brother from your heart" (Mt. 18:21–35). Forgiving others is *not optional.*

7. Think of the person you have the *most* trouble loving. Are you willing to ask God to think of you the way you think of them?

_____

_____

8. Look up Acts 5:31. Besides repentance to Israel, what does Jesus give?

_____

_____

9. Look up Acts 13:38. Why is Jesus preached?

_____

_____

10. Look up Acts 26:18. What is the end result of being transferred from the power of Satan to God?

_____

_____

11. In Ephesians 1:7 and Colossians 1:14, what is the result of redemption through the blood of Christ?

_____

_____

Having been forgiven for everything, we must have hearts that are completely and entirely full of forgiveness for those who have wronged us. But the world is a messy place—what does this *look* like? We usually have a better understanding of forgiveness when receiving it, because we *need* the forgiveness we receive to be all-encompassing. We want to receive forgiveness dispensed from a fire hose, and we want to ladle it out with a teaspoon. But Jesus came to save us from our parsimonious selves. Forgiveness means treating the other person as though they did absolutely no wrong—even though you know that they did do something wrong. Forgiveness presupposes real sin. You don't have to kid yourself to be forgiving—in fact, it is crucial not to. "I'll forgive him because he didn't really mean it" is whitewash, not forgiveness.

This forgiveness means that your heart attitude is that of treating them as though they had done no wrong. Forgiveness doesn't erase certain consequences of sin. For example, a young girl can be forgiven for sleeping with her boyfriend—but she still has the baby.

What are the mechanics of forgiveness? First, love and forgiveness cover a multitude of sins (1 Pet. 4:8). This means that forgiveness (for a certain kind of sin) *can* be extended without the other person's cooperation. But this "cover" has to be a cleansing carpet, not a lumpy one.

12. What sorts of sins might this kind of forgiveness need to cover?

_____

Second, love and forgiveness do not attempt to read the heart (Lk. 17:3–5). We are told to forgive, up to seven times daily, which actually means 490 times, and this applies even though all of us would have our suspicions about the third or fourth time. Forgiveness is a *transaction*, like the sale of a mule. When you forgive someone, it is because they asked you to promise that you would not hold their sin against them, and you extended that promise.

13. What are they asking you to promise, and what are you promising?

_____

_____

Third, love and forgiveness confront when necessary (Mt. 18:15–19). This must only be pursued for the sake of the other person, not your own sake. It is quite striking that Jesus tells the parable of the unmerciful servant immediately after the famous "Matthew 18" instruction. But both these teachings are in Matthew 18. The unmerciful servant is the one sinned against, and so he would have been the one following the Matthew 18 court process.

But conservative believers are far more *comfortable* with accusation than they ought to be. Run a thought experiment concerning two hundred Christian law students who have just passed the bar. One hundred of them are going to be defense attorneys, and one hundred will be prosecutors. Which group will most likely be asked to justify their choice of a profession, and asked how they reconcile it with their Christian faith?

CONFESSION OF SIN

Confession of sin is a basic activity that all Christians need to understand and practice. It is the most fundamental form of spiritual housekeeping.

"If we say that we have no sin, we deceive ourselves, and the truth is not in us. If we confess our sins, he is faithful and just to forgive us our sins, and to cleanse us from all unrighteousness. If we say that we have not sinned, we make him a liar, and his word is not in us" (1 Jn. 1:8–10).

1. What do we do if we say we have no sin?

_____

_____

2. What is not in us if we say we have no sin?

_____

_____

3. What two things happen if we confess our sins?

_____

_____

4. What two attributes of God cause this to happen?

_____

_____

5. What do we say about God if we say we have not sinned?

_____

_____

6. What is not in us?

_____

_____

If we decide to lie to ourselves, then obviously the truth is not in us (v. 8). One of the lies we like to tell ourselves is the lie that our current condition is "normal," and that we have no sin. Or, at least, we have no sin to speak of. John tells us that this is self-deception, period. And if we lie in this way, we are making God into a liar (because He says we *have* sinned), and His word is obviously not in us—a lie is (v. 10).

The meat of this sandwich is in verse 9, but these two pieces of bread make it a sandwich. Don't kid yourself, John is saying—we all need to hear this. Now in the ninth verse John gives us a conditional statement. If we confess our sins, God will do something. The word for confess is *homologeo*, and literally means "to speak the same thing." If we say the same thing about our sin that God says about it (i.e., that it *is* sin), then God will do what He promises. What is that? God will be faithful and just to forgive us our sins, and He will cleanse us from all unrighteousness.

Imagine two mothers with a robust family—six kids each, let's say. One home is bombed all the time and the other is spotless. The difference between the two homes is *not* that in the second home nothing is ever spilled, or knocked over, or left on the coffee table. The difference between the home that is trashed and the home that isn't is the difference between leaving things there "for the present," and picking them up right away.

7. Can the same number of things be spilled or knocked over in two houses, and yet one of the houses is clean and the other filthy?

_____

_____

Given God's promise above, we need to recognize what this means. The promise is good on Monday mornings, and Thursday afternoons. The promise is good in May, and good in October. That means there is never a legitimate reason for refusing to deal with it *now*. The vacuum cleaner is never broken, never at the shop, never too far away, never too hard to operate. The word is near you, in your heart and in your mouth. "God, what I just said to my mother . . . that was sin." *That* is confession. And God's promise is fulfilled at that moment.

The writer to the Hebrews describes what sin does when you leave it unattended. It starts to trip you up—it starts to really get in the way. "Wherefore seeing we also are compassed about with so great a cloud of witnesses, *let us lay aside every weight, and the sin which doth so easily beset us*, and let us run with patience the race that is set before us . . ." (Heb. 12:1). Sin clutters, sin gets in the way, sin weighs you down, sin gets tangled around your feet. Set it aside, we are told, and then run the race.

You can't run the race with a two-hundred-pound backpack on. You cannot run the race with snarls of rope tangled around your feet. Stop trying to be good with unconfessed sin in your life. It just makes you more irritable than you already are. John tells us how to get untangled. Don't try to do that and run at the same time. Get completely untangled, take off the backpack, and *then* run.

So let's change the image. Suppose you haven't cleaned the garage for twenty years, and you are overwhelmed at the very thought of trying to straighten it out. Every time you go open the door, you just stare helplessly at the pile for about five minutes, and then go back inside. All you can think of to do is pray for a fire. Now suppose that is what your pile of unconfessed sin looks like. You are tempted to think that you have to remember everything that is in there first, and then set about cleaning it up. But you don't have to remember the sins you don't remember—the ones on the bottom of the pile. Just confess the ones you *do* remember. The ones you stuffed just inside the garage door just last week. Don't try to remember what is at the bottom of the pile; just look at what is on the top of the pile. If you deal with the sin you know about honestly, then God will cleanse you from *all* unrighteousness. The confessing is your job; the cleansing is His.

8. In the space below, draw a basic graph, with a vertical axis on the left and a horizontal one along the bottom. Alongside the vertical axis, write the word *joy* and along the horizontal axis write *time*. We are going to graph what a lot of Christian lives look like.

Now draw a short line, left to right, of some poor guy sludging along before he becomes a Christian. Then mark the change when he does come to Christ.

So he is now up on the top of his graph, right? Now, as time goes by, draw his line slipping down near the bottom line. Suppose we were to superimpose another graph on top of this one, with the horizontal axis still being time, but the vertical axis is now Bible knowledge or church knowledge. This gives us what we might call the "pretend line" or "praise the Lord" line—a dotted line up near the top. Or at least where everybody else's pretend line is.

Now confession of sin is what restores a man to the place where he was when he first became a Christian. Let's say he does that. He is back up top, right? Now what happens when a couple months go by, and he starts to slide again? He can do the same thing again. A week, and Sunday is tomorrow? He can confess a week's worth on Saturday night. A day? The same thing before bedtime, so he can spend eight hours in fellowship with God sound asleep before he gets up and starts sinning again. Now what is the point? Remember the illustration of the blitzed house. What happens if you pick it up now? What happens on the graph if you confess it now?

On the right side of the graph, you have someone who sins, certainly, but they are still in fellowship with God 99 percent of the time. On the left side, they sin and wallow in it—in fellowship with God 0 percent of the time.

The central virtue here is that of honesty. No blowing smoke at God. No spin control. No attempts to make yourself the flawed hero in this tragic affair. We saw that *homologeo* means "to speak the same." If God calls it adultery, don't you call it an affair or indiscretion. If God calls it grumbling and complaining, don't you call it realism. If God calls it theft, don't you call it shrewd business. As the Puritans might have put it, had they only thought of it, blowing smoke and honest confession accord not well together.

This is not meant to sound flippant. Sin is a ravening wolf, and has destroyed many things. If you have held back from confessing your sins because you know that to do so could threaten your marriage, or cost you your job, or get you expelled from school, you really do have a significant practical problem. I am not saying you should charge off and start confessing your sin like a loose cannon on deck. But you should decide *today* to deal with it honestly, and depending on how tangled up it is, get counsel and help *today* in putting things right. Commit yourself now. Busting yourself is the best thing you can do to rebuild trust with those you may have wronged.

And last, allow me to consider your feelings. You may feel like a hesitant cliff-diver, toes curled over the edge, and here I am poking you in the back with a stick. There are any number of things you might want to do—anything but jump.

9. You might rationalize. "What I did wasn't really wrong." What does it mean if you are walking around, muttering to yourself that what you did was really, really right?

_____

_____

10. You might excuse. "What I did was not started by *me*." This is a variation of "what I did was wrong, *but*." What happens to your forgiveness when you say that magic word *but*?

_____

_____

11. You might postpone it. "In *my* honest opinion, the best day for jumping will be sometime tomorrow afternoon." But what happens when you get to tomorrow afternoon? Is confessing then easier or harder?

_____

_____

12. You might blame somebody else, anybody else. "I think *they* should be here jumping, not me." When you lie, you think about your lie. When someone lies about you, and you get bitter, what comes to mind whenever you think of the situation? But you can confess their sins all day long and not get your joy back.

_____

_____

13. You might use vague terms to try jumping sideways along the cliff edge. "I think that, generally speaking, I have certainly sinned in *some* ways." Or you might say, "I never said I was perfect." Why do you not want to tell God the particular way in which you were imperfect this time?

_____

_____

It is easy to dismiss this kind of emphasis as morbid introspectionism, but actually it is the opposite. If you confess your sins, lay aside the weight of that backpack, you never have to think about it again. Now, with it unconfessed, you think about it frequently. John says that refusal to acknowledge sin is "walking in darkness" (1 Jn. 2:9, 15–17). This can lead to real frustration in dealing with sin. Why? You're in the dark! And as we have already noticed, it can also lead to an outright denial of sin (1 Jn. 1:8, 10).

When you confess sin, as described above, you are walking in the light (1 Jn. 1:7; 2:6). What does walking in the light result in? The first thing is that it results in fellowship with one another.

14. In the space below, draw a triangle with an apex at the top. Put the word *God* there. If you are one of the other corners, what happens when you move along the line toward God, and somebody else on the other corner does the same?

What else happens as a result of walking in the light? We are purified from all sin (1:7). How does this happen? The blood of God's Son, Jesus, does this for us.

Now, how does a Christian leave darkness and enter light? Simple—by simple confession of sin. God, who has no darkness, says something about your sin. Say the same thing that He does. That's it. Do this with whatever He calls sin, and not just with the sins that annoy you. Recognize that this is all based on His justice and faithfulness, not yours. Simply accept and receive His purification of all your sins. And remain walking in the light.

RESTITUTION: THE FORGOTTEN DUTY

Now we have considered forgiveness of sin in some detail. But we have to note that forgiveness of sin is not a redefinition of sin (Rom. 13:8–10). "Christians aren't perfect, just forgiven" contains a glorious truth. But, misapplied as it frequently is, it also represents a travesty of biblical living. Forgiveness of sin does not mean that sin is now okay, or that we get to sin a lot because the grace of God is prompted by sin (Rom. 6:1–3). These issues become enormously practical when we come to the question of restitution, as we now have.

1. Look up Leviticus 6:1–7. In verse 1, who is speaking, and who is being spoken to?

_____

_____

2. In verse 2, when a man wrongs his neighbor in some kind of property transaction, who is he really sinning against?

_____

_____

3. In verse 3, does it matter if a man finds something that belongs to someone else and lies about it afterwards?

_____

_____

4. In the fourth verse, what is the basic duty that he has if he has done this sort of thing?

_____

_____

5. In verse 5, when he restores what he has deceitfully gotten, what does he add to it?

_____

_____

6. Once he has done this, what does he need to do in relation to the Lord, since it is the Lord he has sinned against?

_____

_____

7. Look up Hebrews 10:1–4. Since Jesus has come and died on the cross, is there any need for us to offer a trespass offering?

_____

_____

God is the only ultimate owner of anything. The earth is the Lord's, and the fullness thereof (Ps. 24:1; 1 Cor. 10:26). This is why property sins and crimes are sins against the *Lord* (v. 2). This is what God Himself says (v. 1). Property sins of various kinds can be perpetrated by means of deceit or by violence (v. 2). They can also occur through a windfall, with lying as a follow-up (v. 3). All the kinds of things "that men do" are covered here (v. 3). This is why the law of Moses here would cover computer fraud, even though computers weren't invented yet. The thief must restore what is not his (v. 4). Whatever means he used to filch it, he must return it, along with an additional 20 percent (v. 5). He is then to bring a trespass offering to the Lord (v. 6), and the Lord will forgive him for this kind of sin (v. 7).

In the Old Testament, restitution was accompanied by the guilt offering. In the New Testament, the fact that the sacrifice of Jesus Christ on the cross fulfills the guilt offering does *not* mean that it fulfills the restitution.

In addition, when God prohibited adultery in the Ten Commandments (Exod. 20:14), this presupposed that He had established and defined the institution of marriage. When He says not to steal, this means that He has established and defined the idea of private property (Exod. 20:15). We must reject the Enlightenment idea that property rights are somehow held autonomously—whether by individuals or the state. We "own" *only* what God has given us stewardship over—but if God has granted that stewardship, then it cannot be abrogated by man. Attempts to do so are called stealing—whether by the government or by thieves working in the private sector.

Next, men are stewards not just of "stuff" but are also stewards of time, and the fruitfulness that time makes possible. There is no such thing as static wealth. So when a thief restores the property, he must also restore the time it was gone. This, presumably, is why the 20 percent is not a constant. Sometimes the thief had to pay double (Exod. 22:4, 7).

Now, there are a few objections to this that might come up. We can certainly come up with all kinds of reasons why restitution is not practical for us. For example, we might say that restitution would make the future inconvenient for me. To which the answer should be, *so?*

8. If a thief cannot pay the amount back, what do the Scriptures allow for (Exod. 22:3)?

_____

It appears that this would be inconvenient for the thief, but that is not the point.

9. We might say that we did not *mean* to harm our neighbor's goods. But does the Bible require restitution only if you meant it on purpose? What is required for culpable negligence (Exod. 22:5–6), not just for deliberate theft?

_____

_____

10. We might say that "it broke" when I was borrowing it. What scriptural contingencies distinguish between borrowed and rented (Exod. 22:14)?

_____

_____

11. We might say that we can't make restitution because it is simply impossible to do so. We can't remember who we stole it from, or we can't find them. If so, then where should the money go (Num. 5:5–8)? *We* certainly don't get to keep it.

_____

_____

12. Someone might say that the coming of Jesus has wiped the slate clean, and want this to mean that restitution is not necessary. But how would this apply to the situation Luke describes (Lk. 19:10)? Shouldn't this make restitution a joy?

_____

_____

Time does not make "that twenty dollars" yours. The blood of Christ does not make that twenty dollars yours. Forgetfulness does not make that twenty dollars yours. A deficient view of the Old Testament does not make that twenty dollars yours. The fact that you swiped it from your mom does not make it yours. The fact that the person you took it from never missed it does not make it yours. "Fools mock at making amends for sin, but goodwill is found among the upright" (Prov. 14:9, NIV).

We must remember as Christians that property rights *are* human rights. When economic libertarians try to ground property rights in the autonomous individual, without any reference to Christ, they are making an idol out of property. Whatever good things they might say about economics do not keep this from being an idol, and behaving as idols always do. And one of the things that idols always do is destroy that which is idolized. Those who worship sex destroy it. Those who worship wine destroy it. Those who worship mammon destroy our ability to enjoy it as a very fine fellow creature (1 Tim. 6:17).

We must refuse to worship property, we must refuse to worship our stuff. And this is why stewardship-property can be secure. With autonomous property as the rope, atomistic libertarians will always lose their tug of war with the state. When we compare the secularist (economic) libertarians with the secularist statists, we are looking at the difference between a competent businessman who loves money and an incompetent businessman who loves money. We have no reason to cheer for one over the other Christians are to see property as an incarnational and God-given way *to love other people* (Rom. 13:8). And this leads to our last point, the most important one, really.

13. Look up Ephesians 4:28, and summarize it in your own words.

_____

_____

Hard-liners can pound this text—"Take the money back, you antinomian!"—and miss the point of the law, which is love. What is the greatest commandment? That we love God. What is the second? That we love our neighbor. When the thief repents, he is to get a job—but not so that he can become a fat cat. He is to labor with his hands . . . why? So that he might be able to *give*.

Whenever anyone puts property ahead of people, he is assaulting the reason God gave property to us in the first place. But when others foolishly react to this error, putting people ahead of property, they have abandoned the only material God gave us for loving others. And one of the best ways to recover this understanding is to recover wisdom about restitution.

ASSURANCE OF SALVATION

We are commanded in Scripture to make our calling and election sure (2 Pet. 1:10). It is not a grievous command; being confident in God's salvation is a wonderful frame of mind. God does not want His children to lack an assurance of their standing before Him; He wants us to know what He has given to us. In addition, the question "Am I really a Christian?" is a question that many Christian young people ask themselves. Not surprisingly, this is a question the Bible wants us to know how to ask and answer.

"These things have I written unto you that believe on the name of the Son of God; that ye may know that ye have eternal life, and that ye may believe on the name of the Son of God." (1 Jn. 5:13)

1. According to this passage, why did John write to those who believe?

_____

2. If he wants them to know this, is it reasonable to assume that it is possible to know?

_____

But this does not mean God wants us to be guilty of presumption; He does not want us to rest secure in an imaginary salvation. It is therefore necessary to guard against a false assurance.

"Examine yourselves, whether ye be in the faith; prove your own selves. Know ye not your own selves, how that Jesus Christ is in you, except ye be reprobates?" (2 Cor. 13:5). Implicit in this warning is the assumption that someone could be deceived in the matter. Consequently, Paul tells the Corinthians to double-check in order to make sure that they are genuine Christians.

So the knowledge of how to have a biblical assurance of salvation is greatly needed; it is needed because many genuine Christians do not live with a true assurance of salvation that God can give to us through His Word. The problem of false Christians is one to address another time.

There are a number of things mentioned in Scripture that characterize the lives of those who are genuine Christians. No one of these should be taken in isolation. Together, however, they give us sound indicators of what happens when God has indeed stepped into a person's life.

3. For the first, look up 1 John 3:14. If we love the brethren, what do we therefore know?

_____

That's right—true Christians love other Christians. There is a spiritual kinship between believers which is given by God. This supernatural kinship is a sign that a genuine conversion has occurred. John's statement here is very clear. A Christian's assurance of having passed from death to life is based on his love for the brothers. The other side of the coin is equally clear. Someone who does not love his brothers has not passed out of death.

This scriptural truth has been the experience of many. Before becoming Christians, many people are irritated and bothered by Christians. The believers are seen as self-righteous, judgmental, and hard to be around. But when the individual is converted, the whole picture changes. Suddenly, Christians are a joy to be around. This shows that the person has passed from death to life. He was once an outsider; he is now a member of the family.

4. Not only is this love an evidence to ourselves that we are Christians, it is also an evidence to those around us that we are Christians. Look up what Jesus said in John 13:34–35. If the Christians love each other, what do all men recognize as a result?

_____

Love is the first mark of a Christian. If love is there, an assurance of new life is possible. If love is not there, then neither is salvation. And if salvation is not there, then assurance of salvation is certainly not there.

5. The second mark of a Christian can be seen in 1 John 2:3. We know that we have come to know God if we do something. What is that something?

_____

This mark is obedience. When someone is converted, his lifestyle changes. The change occurs because the person is now serving a new master, and this new master requires and enables the changes to happen.

Again, John's statement is clear. Knowledge of salvation is there if obedience to God's commands is also there. Contextually, this obedience is love. This takes us back to the first mark of assurance we mentioned. However, it also takes us beyond it.

Love is not an emotion, nor is it a tidal wave of gushy feelings. Love can be accompanied by emotion, or the emotion can be lacking. The greatest expression of real love was when Jesus went to the cross for His Church. But He did not, however, go to the cross on an emotional high. Rather, He prayed, "O my Father, if it be possible, let this cup pass from me: nevertheless not as I will, but as thou wilt" (Mt. 26:39b). In the previous verse, He said to the disciples, "My soul is exceeding sorrowful, even unto death" (Mt. 26:38). So, then, we see that Jesus did not have any emotional desire to die for us. How, then, was this an act of love? It was an act of love because Jesus obeyed the Father. "And being found in fashion as a man, he humbled himself, and became obedient unto death, even the death of the cross" (Phil. 2:8).

In the same way, our love is communicated through obedience. We show our love for the Father by what we do. We also show our love for our brothers by what we do. Love dictates and motivates certain actions, and it prohibits others. Love does no harm to its neighbor.

> Owe no man any thing, but to love one another: for he that loveth another hath fulfilled the law. For this, Thou shalt not commit adultery, Thou shalt not kill, Thou shalt not steal, Thou shalt not bear false witness, Thou shalt not covet; and if *there be* any other commandment, it is briefly comprehended in this saying, namely, Thou shalt love thy neighbour as thyself. Love worketh no ill to his neighbour: therefore love *is* the fulfilling of the law (Rom. 13:8–10)

Love can be measured, and the measuring stick is obedience to God's law. But it is important to make a distinction here. Raw obedience will never lead to love. But real love will always result in obedience and can be measured by that obedience.

When love resulting in obedience is present, there is genuine assurance that a person is a genuine Christian. This obedience is not accomplished by our own puny efforts. It does not happen because of our strength. Rather, it is the result of the Holy Spirit's working in us. His presence and help is an additional assurance that we are indeed God's children.

"For if ye live after the flesh, ye shall die: but if ye through the Spirit do mortify the deeds of the body, ye shall live. For as many as are led by the Spirit of God, they are the sons of God" (Rom. 8:13-14).

This does not teach that an attempt to put the misdeeds of the body to death will make you a Christian. Rather, it teaches that misdeeds of the body are put to death by means of the Spirit. If the Spirit is leading you in this way, then you are a child of God.

The third mark of assurance is found in what happens when we disobey. When we disobey God the Father, it does not mean we are no longer His children. On the contrary, if we disobey and God disciplines us, that means we truly are His children. God doesn't spank the neighbor's kids. He spanks His own. This is the clear teaching of the Scripture.

6. Look up Hebrews 12:7–8, and answer this question. When you endure chastening, what is happening?

_____

7. If someone is not chastened, then what does this make him?

_____

The fact that God disciplines us should be a source of encouragement to us. It means we belong to Him. Although painful, it truly is a comfort. This mark also helps place the second mark (obedience) into perspective. The obedient life is not the same thing as the perfect life.

8. Read Hebrews 12:5–6. Chastening is a sign of what?

_____

Has the Lord rebuked you? It means He cares for you. Has He disciplined you? It means He loves you. Has He punished you? It means He considers you His son. It is not impossible for a Christian to sin. It is impossible for a Christian to sin and get away with it.

In the context of Hebrews 12, we see that the Lord's discipline has two aspects. The first is preventative. The Lord allows hardships into our lives (for example, persecution) in order to strengthen us. We have not yet resisted sin to the point of shedding our blood, as the Lord did, but God wants to prepare us for that possibility.

The second aspect is God's response to our sin. When we sin, God punishes us by removing our joy (Gal. 4:15; Ps. 51:12). We are not to lose heart when He rebukes us. Both aspects are grounds of assurance for us.

Perhaps an example may be helpful. If one of my children were to disobey me, he would still be my child. Because he is still my child, he would receive a spanking. The disobedience affects their fellowship with me, but not their relationship to me. In fact, the discipline they receive underlines the fact that the relationship is still intact. In the same way, when we disobey God, our fellowship with Him is affected (we lose the joy of salvation), but our relationship to Him remains intact.

9. The fourth mark of assurance can be found in 1 Corinthians 1:18. Look that passage up, and write down the difference shown between two kinds of people when the cross is preached.

_____

This mark is an understanding of spiritual things. God's children understand spiritual things; beginning with the gospel. If that sort of understanding is lacking, then spiritual life is absent. For someone in a state of spiritual death (Eph. 2:1–2), the message of the cross makes no sense at all. In contrast, the one being saved sees and understands the gospel as being powerful. The power is great and it brings salvation (Rom. 1:16). To the one who is perishing, the death of a Jewish carpenter for the sins of lost humanity is nonsense.

A little later in 1 Corinthians, Paul reinforces this point: "But the natural man receiveth not the things of the Spirit of God: for they are foolishness unto him: neither can he know them, because they are spiritually discerned"(1 Cor. 2:14).

So the unspiritual man does not understand the gospel. Nor does the unspiritual man understand the Bible, the book that brings us the gospel. At the point of conversion, the gospel suddenly makes sense and the Bible turns into English. For religious non-Christians, God-words that they have been familiar with all their lives suddenly become filled with meaning. Before conversion, a man listens to sermons and hears nothing but *yammeryammeryammerJesusyammeryammerbegoodyammer.*

The ability to understand salvation and the cross is something that God gives along with salvation. When that understanding is present, then it brings assurance.

10. The fifth mark has to do with the truth. Look up Romans 10:9. In that passage, someone will be saved if they do two things. What are those two things?

_____

There are certain things which a man cannot deny and be considered a Christian. These are truths that are of first importance. Salvation is linked to one's confession. Obviously, the confession has to come from the heart; verbal recitation is not enough. We are not saying that the preacher's parrot can get saved. While sincerity is necessary (as we saw earlier), a certain doctrinal content is also necessary.

And in another place it says: "Whosoever shall confess that Jesus is the Son of God, God dwelleth in him, and he in God" (1 Jn. 4:15).

The basics of the faith that must be acknowledged have to do with who Jesus is and what He did on the cross for us. A man who is faithful to the message of the cross can be assured of salvation.

11. Look up John 5:24. If a man hears the words of Jesus, and believers on the Father who sent Him, what does he have?

_____

12. What will he not come into?

_____

13. And why will that not happen?

_____

A man who denies it, or who holds to it nominally, does not have that salvation. It is not enough to bear the name Christian. The gospel must be understood and believed. The object of faith, the message of Christ, has a certain content to be believed. One who believes and believes correctly, can come before God with confidence. Salvation and the content of the salvation message cannot be separated.

"Beloved, when I gave all diligence to write unto you of the common salvation, it was needful for me to write unto you, and exhort you that ye should earnestly contend for the faith which was once delivered unto the saints" (Jude 3).

We now come to the sixth mark of assurance. Our God is a giving God. In the cross, God gave His Son for the sins of mankind. At Pentecost, God gave His Spirit to the Church. When regeneration occurs, God has given His Spirit to the individual. This giving of the Spirit is another means that God uses to give assurance to His children.

14. Look up 1 John 4:13. If God has given us His Spirit, then what two things do we know as a consequence?

_____

Receiving the Spirit (in this sense) is synonymous with becoming a Christian. When the Spirit has taken up residence, He makes Himself known in a number of ways. One of the most important ways is how the Spirit leads the new child of God in his relationship with God the Father through Jesus Christ (Eph. 2:18).

For ye have not received the spirit of bondage again to fear; but ye have received the Spirit of adoption, whereby we cry, Abba, Father. The Spirit itself beareth witness with our spirit, that we are the children of God (Romans 8:15–16).

"And because you are sons, Paul states this same truth elsewhere: "And because ye are sons, God hath sent forth the Spirit of his Son into your hearts, crying, Abba, Father. Wherefore thou art no more a servant, but a son; and if a son, then an heir of God through Christ" (Gal. 4:6–7).

15. When the Spirit is given to a man, what does He make that man want to cry out?

_____

16. And what would this seem to indicate?

_____

When a man is born again, he is born into a new relationship with God as his Father. This relationship is made possible by the Holy Spirit who motivates us to cry out to the Father. The Spirit provides us with an internal assurance of our standing with God. Because of His presence, we can know that our relationship with the Father is secure.

Because of this relationship, and because the Spirit molds us more and more into the image of Christ (Rom. 8:13–14, 26–29), we can be confident that He will finish what He has begun. In fact, Christians are predestined to Christ-likeness because of the Spirit's work. Thus, the Holy Spirit is our guarantee that this will be accomplished.

". . . after that ye believed, ye were sealed with that holy Spirit of promise, Which is the earnest of our inheritance until the redemption of the purchased possession, unto the praise of his glory." (Eph. 1:13–14)

And in another place: "Now he that hath wrought us for the selfsame thing is God, who also hath given unto us the earnest of the Spirit." (2 Corinthians 5:5)

The result of this guarantee is confidence or assurance on our part (2 Cor. 5:6). Of course it is unthinkable that the Holy Spirit of God could take possession of a person's life and not be able to manifest the fruit of His character in that person's life. And this brings us full circle to the first assurance we discussed, the manifestation of love.

"But the fruit of the Spirit is love, joy, peace, longsuffering, gentleness, goodness, faith, meekness, temperance . . ." (Gal. 5:22–23).

When the Holy Spirit is there, His presence is obvious. Assurance is not based on subjective feelings. It is based on the objective Word of God and the objective changes that the Spirit brings about. The Word of God is a message of love, and the Spirit works that message into our hearts. "And hope maketh not ashamed; because the love of God is shed abroad in our hearts by the Holy Ghost which is given unto us" (Rom. 5:5).

17. So then, in summary, what are the six marks of a true Christian?

_____

_____

_____

_____

_____

_____

RESISTING TEMPTATION

Temptation is a nuisance, and as Christians we look forward to the day when we will be free from temptation. But in the meantime, we must prepare ourselves to resist temptation effectively. Often Christians are unaware of God's promises for times of temptation. We do not experience victory because we misunderstand God's character. Some think that although God knows our dilemma, He has made no promise of deliverance, or they think God has made promises He does not fulfill. In either case, God's character is seriously misunderstood.

In this section, we will cover two biblical truths concerning temptation. First, God calls us to avoid sin. He has given both the command and power to keep us from sin. Secondly, ignorance of this first truth is a very common cause of sin in Christians. This ignorance has various forms which will be discussed.

So what does God desire for us? In 1 Corinthians 10:13, Paul tells us this: "There hath no temptation taken you but such as is common to man: but God is faithful, who will not suffer you to be tempted above that ye are able; but will with the temptation also make a way to escape, that ye may be able to bear it."

1. According to this passage, will God ever allow us to be locked up in temptation, with no way out except by sinning?

_____

So there is no such thing as an impossible temptation. God has promised a way out of every tempting situation—and the promise is linked to the faithfulness of God. In other words, if there is such a thing as temptation with no escape, then we would be justified in accusing God of unfaithfulness. Since unfaithfulness in God is an impossibility, then there must be a way out of every temptation.

2. Jesus instructs us to pray Look up Matthew 6:13, and write down what He expects us to pray for there.

_____

Not only is God willing to keep us from sin, He is also willing to spare us from much of temptation. Many times, the only thing keeping this blessing from us is our unwillingness to believe God. He tells us to pray to keep temptation at a distance, and we should take Him at His word. Much of temptation should not be so much resisted, as avoided. God is willing to help us avoid it, but He requires us to ask for it.

3. What are we told to ask for in Hebrews 4:16?

_____

God extends mercy when we sin. But He also provides grace for our time of need. When we are tempted, He is there. Perhaps it would help to picture sin as a huge, jagged cliff. God in His mercy has parked an ambulance at the bottom (1 Jn. 1:9) in case we fall off, which we have already addressed. But in His grace, He has also built a fence. This fence is His willingness to help us in times of temptation.

In these verses we see God's desire to keep us away from sin. But this desire of His is not strapped on our backs as a burden. It is communicated to us in an offer of help. It is an expression of God's gracious love for us.

4. In Titus 2:11–12, what does Paul tell us about what the grace of God teaches?

_____

So God wants to teach us how to say no to sin (i.e., to deny ungodliness). His grace has been made available to provide that instruction. The least we can do is respond to that grace with willing, teachable hearts. In all these passages (and in many others), we see that God has clearly revealed to us His desire to help us in times of temptation. Why then do many Christians live lives of frustration and defeat? As was mentioned earlier, the problem lies with human ignorance of God's power to deliver and His desire to deliver. What forms can this ignorance take?

The first problem is moral defeatism. Within Christian circles, we commonly find the assumption that God cannot be really pleased with our lives "this side of Jordan." That is, as long as we are on this earth, God cannot be really pleased with us because sin and rebellion against God is somehow inevitable. "God forbid. How shall we, that are dead to sin, live any longer therein?" (Rom. 6:2). In the same chapter, Paul states: "For sin shall not have dominion over you: for ye are not under the law, but under grace" (Rom. 6:14). Grace means freedom from sin, not freedom to sin. In another place Peter tells us: "But as he which hath called you is holy, so be ye holy in all manner of conversation" (1 Pet. 1:15).

The Bible does not permit us to think that God is perpetually angry with us. It is possible to please God. "Furthermore then we beseech you, brethren, and exhort you by the Lord

Jesus, that as ye have received of us how ye ought to walk and to please God, so ye would abound more and more" (1 Thess. 4:1). The Thessalonians were taught to please God, and they learned the lesson well. They had been taught to please God throughout the course of their lives, and they were actually doing so.

5. Look up Proverbs 15:8. What does it say about the upright?

_____

6. And now look up Zephaniah 3:17. What does God rejoice over there?

_____

God will not be fully satisfied with us until His final purpose for us is accomplished (Rom. 8:28–29). But He can be fully pleased with us as we allow Him to remove sin from our lives and we begin to grow. He wants it done now, and His delight should be motivation enough. God is easy to please, but hard to satisfy.

The opposite problem is perfectionism, the opposite of defeatism. The perfectionist fails to realize that even though we are new creatures in Christ, our flesh is still fallen. For those in Christ, the old man is crucified, but the flesh still remains with us. The flesh presents the Christian with a constant problem.

7. Look up Romans 6:12. What are Christians there told to not let happen?

_____

Paul is addressing Christians, and he tells them not to let sin reign in their bodies. He goes on and defines "sin reigning" as obeying the lusts of the body. In the phrase "its lusts," the pronoun "its" refers back to the body, and not to sin. In other words, when Christians obey the lusts of the body, the lusts of the flesh, then sin is reigning in their bodies. But if they say no, then those same bodies can be a holy and acceptable sacrifice to God (Rom. 12:1–2).

Because the perfectionist believes that he can attain total and absolute perfection in this life, he does not take into account the remaining corruption and fallenness of his flesh. The flesh is not seen as unredeemed and full of lustful turbulence; it is seen as innocent and neutral.

The end result of all perfectionism is a redefinition of sin. This is because of a missing biblical understanding of the process of redemption; our bodies will not be redeemed until the day of resurrection. Because of God's free justification of His saints, and because He has made us new creatures, He can be fully pleased with how we live our lives before Him. It is here that the defeatist misses the biblical truth. But because our bodies are not yet conformed to the image of Jesus Christ, we must constantly restrain the lusts and desires of the flesh. It is at this point that the perfectionist misses an important biblical truth.

Another point of confusion is that many Christians confuse temptation with sin. But it is not a sin to be tempted. If it were, our Lord would have been a sinner (Mt. 4:1–11).

8. Look up Hebrews 2:18. Who is tempted there?

_____

9. Now look up Hebrews 4:15. In how many ways was Jesus tempted?

_____

Our Lord was tempted but never sinned. Because He was tempted, He is able to sympathize with us in our vulnerability to temptation. Because He never sinned, His sympathy can accomplish something for us through His intercession. Jesus was tempted in the same way we are. Yet those temptations did not bring sin into His life. Neither does it have to bring sin into our lives.

In spite of this truth, many Christians assume that temptation "equals" sin. If an evil suggestion is made, they assume that it came, not from the tempter, but from themselves. It is an easy mistake to make since the source of many of our temptations are not visible to us. But God knows our limitations, and has given us some needed information. "For we wrestle not against flesh and blood, but against principalities, against powers, against the rulers of the darkness of this world, against spiritual wickedness in high places" (Eph. 6:12).

What is the use of putting on the armor of God if the enemy is inside the armor? The armor is there to keep the enemy out, not lock the enemy in.

When we are tempted, the suggestion commonly comes from outside. The fact that the tempter is invisible to us does not alter this truth. God wants us to confess our sins. But it is not necessary to confess our temptations. We should feel free to call upon God for strength in temptation. But it is not good to feel guilty simply because a devil has made a suggestion. Such guilt is false guilt and should be resisted as a separate temptation.

Suppose a man is walking down the street minding his own business, and some foul thought enters his mind. It would be easy to think that the thought had burbled up from his own murky subconscious. No. If his sins were confessed, and he was (up to that point) walking in the light, then the thought is not his responsibility and should be rejected. Think of resisting temptation as playing tennis with the devil. You don't lose points if the ball comes on your side of the net. You lose points if it stays on your side of the net.

When temptation occurs, use God's gracious provision and say no. This needs to be done immediately (within seconds). If a Christian is successful in returning "the ball," the chances are good that he may stand there feeling pretty good about himself. But he needs to be careful; the opposition knows how to volley. First thing he knows, the ball's in his court again, and he is unprepared for it. When Christians resist temptation successfully, it is important not to let down the guard. "Wherefore let him that thinketh he standeth take heed lest he fall" (1 Cor. 10:12).

God needs to protect us in our successes as well as our failures. But suppose someone keeps returning the ball, and it keeps coming back at him. All day long he battles with a recurring temptation. He says no to the same temptation all day. Under such circumstances, it would be easy for him to think of himself as a poor Christian. But that's not poor Christianity; it's good tennis! Remember, there is no sin in being tempted. Our Lord was tempted, and a servant is not greater that his master. Christians will be tempted too, sometimes repeatedly.

Sometimes Christians confuse the weariness that comes from successfully resisting temptation with the discouragement that comes when we sin. They drag home at the end of a long day, tired of being lied to and tired from saying no. It is easy to feel discouraged but the feeling should be resisted. It was probably one of the best days they ever had. They are simply battle weary!

As Martin Luther put it, you can't keep birds from flying over your house, but you can keep them from nesting in your chimney.

To believe that temptation is sin is to malign God's character as manifested in Christ. If temptation is sin, then Christ was a sinner. And if Christ was a sinner then we are still lost in our sins.

Another way to misunderstand God's character in regard to temptation is to consider God-given desires as sins. For example, gluttony is a sin, but biological hunger is not. Sexual immorality is sinful, but having a sexual drive is not. Sin occurs when our desires are gratified (mentally or physically) outside the boundaries that God has established for us. When the boundaries are crossed, then our desires are gratified at someone else's expense. But having those desires is not the problem.

10. Even though these built-in desires are not inherently sinful, they can be used, quite effectively, to draw us into sin. This is to be expected. The Bible gives Christians many repeated warnings about the lusts of the flesh. For just one example, look up 1 Peter 2:11. What wars against the soul?

Temptation occurs when there is a desire to gratify that lust in violation of God's Word. In such situations, we should resist the suggestion without rejecting the desire itself.

11. When we are tempted, we shouldn't blame God for it. Look up James 1:13–15. Who does not draw us into temptation? And what draws us away into temptation?

_____

God does not tempt us. When we are tempted, our desires are used against us by the tempter. In that context, if we gratify our desire, our desires are lusts; we have given birth to sin. Let us not reject the desires God has given, but rather, we should refuse to gratify them outside the will of God. Anything less would reject God's gifts to us and malign His character. "Every good gift and every perfect gift is from above, and cometh down from the Father of lights, with whom is no variableness, neither shadow of turning" (Jas. 1:17).

When some of the Israelites returned to Jerusalem under the leadership of Nehemiah, they faced two problems. One was the hostile nations around them who threatened military action. The second was the construction of the city wall. Scripture tells us how they dealt with both problems.

12. Look up Nehemiah 4:17–18. What two instruments did each Israelite have?

_____

The Israelites were prepared to fight the enemy, which can be compared to fighting off temptation. But they were also willing to work to make themselves less vulnerable to attack. The story provides us with a good picture to illustrate that kind of preparation against temptation. Imagine that a man's personality is a city wall.

13. The comparison is made in Proverbs 25:28. What is a man without self-control compared to?

_____

At some points the wall is strong, and at other points weak. The temptation is the attacking army. Where is he attacked? The answer is obvious: where he is weak.

One man's personality is such that he would never gamble away his paycheck. There his wall is strong. Consequently, he is not attacked there. But in resisting sexual temptation his walls are in shambles. And it seems that the gaps in the walls are always filled with attacking armies. So he positions all his resources there, and he fights, and fights, and fights some more. Perhaps a lesson could be learned from Nehemiah. When attacked, it is important to be prepared for the fight. But between battles, a man should occupy himself with building up the walls. He doesn't have to be so vulnerable to that temptation for the rest of his life. He should build the wall and pray preventively. When he fights, he should have a trowel by his side. When he works, he should have a sword by his side.

Feeding on God's Word is an important part of building the wall, which we will consider in the next lesson. The same applies to prayer and fellowship with other Christians. However, Christians shouldn't approach these things in a legalistic spirit, but rather as the natural means of growth and grace that God has provided. The stronger the wall gets, the easier it will get to resist the old temptations. When that happens, we must look for fresh fighting to break out at another point on the wall—and turn and do the same there. But we must not despair! A seasoned warrior faces the battle with confidence and hope, and in our case, we know who ultimately wins.

How can we sum up what has been said so far? What are the various stages we should consider as we seek to avoid sin? The first thing is to avoid temptation: it is not necessary to go through every temptation. We must pray as Jesus instructed, and live in a manner consistent with that prayer. Lead us not into temptation. When temptation comes, we should flee temptation: even if temptation is encountered, it is not always necessary to resist it. Sometimes it is best to just run away. Paul tells Timothy, "Flee also youthful lusts" (2 Tim. 2:22). This is the strategy that Joseph employed in regard to Potiphar's wife. He ran away (Gen. 39:12). Nothing wrong with that. Third, we are to resist temptation: when temptation cannot be avoided, it is time to resist. "Therefore take up the whole armor of God, that you may be able to withstand in the evil day, and having done all, to stand" (Eph. 6:13). We should meet the temptation head on, fully expecting God to give the victory. Next, we should be steadfast in temptation. Often the temptation won't leave at our first resistance. We have to be prepared to resist until the temptation ceases. It will cease eventually. Many Christians think the only way to make the temptation cease is to submit to it. On the contrary: "Therefore submit to God. Resist the devil and he will flee from you" (Jas. 4:7). The promised victory may not be immediate, but it will come soon enough. Hang on until it does. And last, when the temptation ceases, use time wisely: Christians should prepare and strengthen themselves for the next time they are tempted in that same area. We must build up our city walls.

INTELLIGENT BIBLE READING

The foundation of all true Christian understanding is found in the Bible—and you get this understanding by hearing and by reading. It is safe to say this in the light of the clear teaching of the Bible on the subject.

1. Look up Deuteronomy 8:3. What is the basis of man's life? What is not?

_____

But zealous young Christians who are serious about their faith can easily fall into the trap of studying the Bible before they read it. They may become such great "students" that they never get around to reading it at all. Unfortunately, this pattern is sometimes reinforced by some of the techniques for Bible reading that are commonly taught.

Our text in Deuteronomy says that man lives by every word that comes from God. We do not live by isolated words, words out of context, or words that have been twisted out of all recognition. So all forms of proper Bible study must be preceded by Bible reading, and lots of it. Before outlining a biblical approach to the Bible, perhaps it will be helpful to point out some common problems encountered by young Christians in this regard.

Scripture memory programs can be good, provided the one memorizing looks the verse up in context, and reads what went before, and what comes after. But it is very easy to memorize a verse without considering the context. The one who memorizes Scripture in this way has no idea what the verse is about. The little white card containing the verse has no context.

The results of this can be embarrassing; verses can easily be memorized out of their biblical context. For just a few examples, James 1:5 does not refer to a general request for wisdom, Romans 8:27 has nothing to do with a general pattern of prayer, and the prayer of the disciples in Luke 17:5 for increased faith should not be imitated by us.

2. Suppose you are praying about whether to ask a girl to marry you. You pray and open your Bible at random to Jeremiah 16:1–2. What does God tell you there?

_____

Consider a man who has been a Christian for about three weeks. Would it be possible, over the course of a weekend, for him to memorize twenty-five verses? Certainly, and suppose he then moved to a new city, joined a church where no one knew how long he had been a Christian, and at an appropriate time said, "Well, as it says in Hosea 6:1 . . ." How would others respond to him? They would be thinking that he ought to teach Sunday school, or something. This kind of Bible study without Bible reading can create a dangerous illusion of maturity.

Bible study guides (like this one!) have a series of questions on various topics, and a Bible reference is supplied with each question. After the question is a blank to fill in. These guides are useful (especially this one), if the student is careful to check the context of the passages he looks up. But that involves quite a bit of work, and it may not be possible to get the lesson done in time. Isn't it easier just to supply the answer the question is obviously looking for? And if the biblical context is not ever read, is it not possible to get the answer wrong? For just one example:

3. Why did Jesus say it is important to visit your optometrist regularly (Mt. 6:22–23)?

_____

The expected answer to this question is actually contained in the question, and not in the text. So that is something to be very careful with. These guides are a lot like Ranger Bob's nature trail around the edge of some great wilderness area. Taking in the view at a scenic lookout does not qualify one to call himself a mountain man.

Haphazard "devotional" reading also causes problems. There are many Christians who simply read and reread short favorite passages from the Bible (Ps. 23, or 1 Cor. 13). But suppose someone went to college and studied this way. Take any subject as an example; what would happen to a student who studied history the way many Christians study the Bible? The answer is straightforward; he would flunk. Imagine what would happen when the instructor asks if he has read the assigned chapters, and the student replies, "No, but I particularly like the last paragraph on page 273 of my history text. I return to it often for comfort."

So what should you do? Those who would be well-versed in the teaching of the Bible should simply read their Bibles, cover to cover, again and again, for the rest of their lives. To many this may sound overwhelming. It is not that big a book.

Just read. We should read the Bible like we would read a newspaper or a novel. There is no need to worry about what is being missed. Far more is being gained than lost, and besides, what is missed can be picked up the next time through. You are coming back through soon, right?

Recognize the task is not monumental. Eight pages a day will take the reader through the New Testament once a month. It is not an immense book. The task is even less imposing when it is begun as a task of reading, and not of intense study. Many never begin to read because they think they have an obligation to study the Bible in depth, and they don't know how to do that. They think that in order to read it at all, they have to wring it out like a washcloth. But the task is one of reading; young Christians should not seek to run before they can walk.

Keep track of where you are. There are Bible reading records available, which can be placed in the Bible. When a chapter is read, it is marked off. This helps to ensure that the entire Bible is read (although not necessarily in order of Genesis to Revelation), and keeps the reader from selecting a few favorite bits and pieces. The reader knows what he has read, and how often he has read it.

Select a base translation: my preference is the King James Version—it is a good translation, based on good manuscripts, although it is somewhat creaky. But once the student has a base translation, it is good to read that translation every other time. In between, the translations read can vary. For example: KJV, ESV, KJV, Phillips, KJV, NKJV, KJV . . . The advantage of this is that it keeps the reader from getting into a routine of reading which lures him into paying less attention to what is on the page. People who drive the same route to work every day will sometimes find themselves driving the route on "autopilot." If someone reads the Bible regularly, it is good to read the same passages out of different translations—it helps him to think about what he is reading. When you are writing something down on the notepaper of your brain, it jogs your elbow.

Now as you begin to read, you will soon discover that you have many questions. This is good, because they are *your* questions, and they were generated by the text. As you begin the process of answering these questions from the Bible, you are engaged in true Bible study. You are exhibiting the nobility of the Bereans.

4. Look up Acts 17:11, and answer the following question. What two things exhibited the nobility of the Berean Christians?

The first few times through the Bible, you are imply gaining an understanding of the basic characters, history, and teaching of the Scriptures. You are getting the big picture; you are finding out that Paul lived after King David. But after you have become acquainted with the Bible generally, you are ready to begin asking more detailed questions. When you get to this point, there are several things you can do which will be a help.

First, keep a notebook. The notebook is to record text-generated questions. As you continue reading, you will have many of them answered naturally, and can check them off. But you will also keep adding new questions. For example: "Why does Paul say we are justified apart from works of the law, while James says that faith without works is dead?" "Why did it say here that Judas died by hanging himself and there it says that he died by bursting open?"

Second, keep a section for questions generated from outside the text. Questions like this are those caused by sermons, books, doctrinal positions of friends, etc. For example: "Fred says I should be speaking in tongues. Should I be?" "My non-Christian cousin says that Jesus never claimed to be God. Is that true?"

Third, expect all such questions to be answered by the text. But suppose someone reads the Bible through many times, and he still doesn't find the answer to the question. Then the conclusion should be that the question should never have been asked. If we really need to know the answer, then the Bible has the answer.

This procedure of asking questions, and keeping them in mind as one reads through the Bible, is an acknowledgment of a basic principle of biblical interpretation. Scripture must interpret Scripture.

Now there are some questions which can best be answered from outside the text. In order to help address such questions, the best thing to do is build a library of more objective reference helps. (Interpretive reference helps, such as commentaries, will be discussed later.) Such reference helps include things like a concordance, a Bible software program, a Bible atlas, and portions of a good Bible dictionary. (I say "portions," because it depends on the subject of the entry. Some entries are interpretive, while others are not matters of debate among Christians. For example, I would place the entries on *baptism* and *shekel* in these respective categories.)

These objective reference helps will aid in answering all those questions which cause no interpretive disagreement among Christians. For example: "Where was Galilee?" "What is an ephod?" "Where is the verse that says . . .?"

When one comes to the study of the text itself, the first question to ask of the text should be, "What does it say?" and not, "What does it mean?" At all times the student should be suspicious of all interpretive questions which cannot be answered in the text.

5. Consider the importance of 1 Corinthians 4:6. What did Paul want the Corinthians to learn?

_____

It is the neglect of this truth which produces Wesleyans, Lutherans, Calvinists, Arminians, etc. I am not, of course, rejecting any truth that is held by such groups, but rather the all-too-common "party spirit" which causes a greater allegiance to be given to the group than to the Scriptures. But unfortunately, the factional spirit does not go away just because someone insists upon calling himself a Christian.

6. Which party was the superfactional party in 1 Corinthians 1:12?

_____

When addressing questions of the text, it is important to ask good questions: "Who is speaking here, and to whom? What is the main verb? What was the point of the previous verses?" And so forth.

Bad questions are those which cannot be answered from the text. For example: "Why does the writer choose this word?" "How would you have felt if you were Peter?" "What does this verse mean to you?" "Why do you think . . .?"

Such questions may cause vigorous discussions at the Bible study, but that is not the goal. The goal is to find out what the Bible says.

We come now to the role of interpretive commentary. But in order to begin studying comments on Scripture, it is important to start with the central commentary on Scripture—which is Scripture. We shall look at uninspired commentary later.

The Bible student should get a copy of the Bible he is willing to mark up. Then as he reads the New Testament, he should mark all Old Testament quotations in the New Testament. He may then turn to the Old Testament and mark all the passages which were quoted in the New Testament. This will enable him to use the New Testament as a divinely inspired commentary on the passages of the Old Testament which he has been studying. For example, if he is reading through Hosea, he will come to 11:1. He will see that he has marked that verse as one quoted in Matthew 2:15. He may then turn to Matthew for inspired commentary on Hosea. It is crucial to remember that if the question has not been answered in the text, then it has not really been answered at all. Any answer we give apart from the teaching of the Bible is only our speculation.

It is also important to remember that there are various concentric circles of context for any verse. They are: the verse itself, the passage containing the verse, the book containing the passage, other passages cited by the passage, other books by the same author, the rest of that testament, the rest of the Bible, and the surrounding culture of the writer

There is another important component in understanding the Bible, which is obedience. George MacDonald once said that obedience is the great opener of eyes. Biblical understanding that is not lived out in a practical way is worse than useless. James warns us that a man who hears the word but does not do it is a self-deceiver (Jas. 1:21). He only thinks his knowledge is increasing; it is not. The whole point of Bible study is application to our lives.

7. Like certain men of Issachar (1 Chr. 12:32), we should know how the Word applies to the current situation. What were they able to do?

_____

As the Bible is read and studied, a prime concern should be to discover what duties are assigned, what their doctrinal foundation is, and in what arena the duty should be discharged.

Obedience begins with an attitude. It is the attitude which says, "When the meaning of the text is clear to me, I will immediately put what I have learned into practice in my life."

But we must not obey before we understand the text; we must not delay when we understand the text. For example, does obedience to Matthew 5:29–30 require self-mutilation? If someone charges off to obey the text before they understand it, he will probably live to regret it.

This sort of immediate obedience will in turn increase your understanding of Scripture, leading to further obedience. We must always keep in mind that obedience to the clear teaching of Scripture is the heart of biblical studies. The point of all such study should be to increase ability to obey. If it is not oriented this way, then all the Bible study in the world will be nothing more than a hobby—like stamp collecting. Always beware of such foolishness.

Biblical theology is the truth of Scripture presented in the language of Scripture, and in the manner of Scripture. But learning to think and speak biblically is not necessarily simple.

8. Look up 2 Peter 3:15–16. What do unstable people do to the Scriptures, and what is the result?

_____

The Bible is not written in easy-to-understand outline form, ready-made for professional and amateur theologians. The Scripture is composed of law, teaching, poetry, prophecy, apocalyptic literature, and so forth. In the text above, Peter referred to Scripture that was hard to understand, and he was referring primarily to a portion that is straight didactic teaching.

This means that believing interpretation is not the same thing as simplistic interpretation. But this presents a question. Evangelical Christians frequently encounter the objection from non-Christians that we take the Bible literally. What is the answer to this?

The answer is that a literalistic one-size-fits-all interpretation is not what we apply. Nor do we apply a spiritual interpretation or an allegorical interpretation. The Bible is to be interpreted naturally. Any given passage or book must be interpreted the way it presents itself to be interpreted.

So the text itself should determine how it is to be handled. The following are just a few examples.

Literal: Luke presents his book to the reader as sober history, and those who take the Bible seriously will take it as sober history. To take what is presented literally in a symbolic way distorts the text.

9. Look up Luke 1:2–4. How should we take what he wrote?

_____

Symbolic: The apostle John has given us a glorious vision of the New Jerusalem.

10. Look up Revelation 21:9–12. What indication of symbolism is there?

_____

So does this mean the New Jerusalem comes down from Heaven like the space shuttle? No, we must consider what he says in verses 9–11; he tells us there that the New Jerusalem is the bride of the Lamb—it is a wonderful symbol of the Christian church. To take what is presented symbolically in a literal way distorts the text.

Poetry and figures of speech: Jesus said he was the door (Jn. 10:7). With doorknobs? The Lord is my shepherd. Really? Must we eat grass on all fours to be good Christians? These examples are comical, but great errors have come about through failure to recognize figures of speech in the Bible.

The Bible comes to us in normal human language. It therefore contains all the variations of expression common to language. To forget that the Word of God comes to us in ordinary language distorts the text. We can distort things by taking literal things symbolically, or by taking symbolic things literally. Suppose you were talking to your neighbor, an international student who had been here just a few weeks, and who still had to carry a pocket dictionary with him. You told him you had a rough weekend because of all the rain. "Why?" he asks. Because, you say, you got cabin fever. You know, you were climbing the walls. You know, stir crazy. You know, you were beside yourself. You know, the whole family was going nuts.

Now someone who reads the Bible through, again and again, studying those aspects of the Word which are a puzzle, and putting into practice what is understood, should be able to begin to concentrate on certain books of the Bible: "The basic argument of Paul in Romans is . . ." "Revelation is a series of visions which portray . . ."

It is here that commentaries, books, and expository preachers can be a great supplemental help. But it is important not to limit oneself to just one author or commentator—however good he is. As a result of ongoing reading and study, patterns of thought and speech will become more and more biblical. Also, there is protection against the simplistic mistake which regards the Bible as a solitary unit, with a standard vocabulary. For example, how is the word "lion" used (Rev. 5:5; 1 Pet. 5:8)?

Biblical theology is always overtly contextual. As such, discussions in biblical theology will be connected to specific passages and books, and perhaps to an author. The Bible is read contextually, and it is applied contextually.

So what about systematic theology? That is the practice of presenting biblical truth in the context of all of Scripture. The immediate context of the various passages must be respected, but that immediate context is not in the forefront of the discussion. Paul was referring to a systematic theology when he said, "For I have not shunned to declare unto you all the counsel of God" (Acts 20:27).

Systematic theology presents an abstract of the teaching of the entire Bible on a particular issue. When someone says, "The Bible teaches . . . ," he is doing systematic theology, whether formal or informal. Systematic theology summarizes the teaching of the entire Bible on a particular issue, and presents it in the abstract. There are different ways to do this. They include: creeds, confessions, statements of faith, formal systematics written by theologians, and other representations of the entire Bible's teaching (as in sermons).

But there is still danger. Systematic theologies are a lot like CliffsNotes. In the presence of a systematic theology, it is perilously easy for those who want easy answers to obtain those answers without going to the Bible. Those who are impatient and must have immediate answers may fall to the same temptation. It is easy to read CliffsNotes without reading the book, and it looks to others as though the book has been read. The same abuse is common with the various forms of systematics. It is deadly.

Some have reacted to this abuse by saying that we should stick to biblical theology. But this makes it impossible to summarize and represent what the Bible says on a particular subject. The passages which teach the deity of Jesus Christ are not all found together; they are scattered throughout the Bible. This means that the basic Christian confession—Jesus is Lord—cannot be made apart from systematics.

It is quite true that systematic theologies can be wrong. Because they can be wrong (and many of them are), it is important to be well grounded in the Bible first. As we have discussed, this is accomplished through Bible reading. Otherwise, it is possible to pick up a preconception which is not biblical, and assume it to be true whenever one does read the Bible. For example, how long will the Great Tribulation at the end of the world be? Seven years? Well, that is according to one systematic theology (dispensationalism). But there are other ways to understand it.

Properly done, systematic theology is understanding the whole counsel of God. As a Christian develops a systematic theology, he is asking, and answering, such questions as, "Was Jesus Christ fully God?" The answer is yes, but the answer is found throughout Scripture.

"Was He fully human?" Yes again, but the answer is not based on one or two proof texts.

"Does God foreordain and control all things?" Still yes, but this is a question which generates many more questions—which in turn must be answered from all of Scripture.

"Is God triune?" The God of the Bible is a Holy Trinity; the source of this faith is the entire Bible, which is read, studied, and summarized.

Where possible, our vocabulary in systematics should be determined by the Bible; it should be a biblical vocabulary. There are many such available words: covenant, propitiation, justification, regeneration, and so forth.

Unless the goal is to confuse people, it is important not to coin new words for things that have no set word in Scripture. There is an important humility in using the vocabulary that has developed in the church over the last two thousand years. We are not the first to grapple with these issues. For example, take the word "Trinity." This is a word which is not found in the Bible (of course, "biblical" is not found in the Bible either), but it clearly expresses and summarizes a truth of Scripture.

The process of learning the teaching of the Bible is not a complex one. We begin very simply; we read and reread the Bible. As we read, we begin to ask and answer questions from the text. Objective questions, not dealing with interpretation, can be answered with various resource tools.

As soon as the teaching of the Bible becomes clear to us at a particular point, obedience is necessary. Otherwise, we are simply storing God's truths in the dusty attics of our brains. As we continue to read, we begin developing a biblical theology, based on the biblical context. And lastly, but not therefore less important, we must come to a systematic theology. If we want to have our roots sink deeply into the soil of Scripture, then we must never stop until the fruit we bear is an understanding of the whole counsel of God.

PLEASANT WORDS

Messages on the tongue can easily cause every Christian to respond with some sort of "uh-oh." We all know how readily we sin with the tongue, and if a preacher is aiming for conviction it is fairly easy to hit that target through preaching on "sins of the tongue." But we all know, whether we receive reminders or not, that gossip, cattiness, lying, spin control, tale-bearing, and any other such things, are sins to be confessed and forsaken. But let us suppose we have cast this demon out, and the house is swept and furnished. What happens next? In other words, it is not enough to avoid bad words.

The power of the tongue is enormous, but many Christians imagine this to be the power of dynamite, randomly thrown about. The power is thought to be simply *destructive*; constructive uses are scarcely to be imagined. But this is not the biblical emphasis at all. The power of the tongue to do good is clearly attested throughout the Scriptures. Let's consider what the speaking of good words means.

1. So, look up Proverbs 16:21–24. In verse 21, who is known as prudent?

_____

2. Notice the general flow in this passage, which is heart to mouth. What results from sweetness of the lips?

_____

3. Wisdom in the heart leads to sweetness on the lips, which in turn causes others to learn (v. 21). What, like wisdom, is also in the heart, and is described as a wellspring of life, bubbling up (v. 22)?

_____

4. But what bubbles up out of the heart of the fool?

_____

5. What instructs the mouth of a wise man (v. 23)?

_____

6. Moreover, what does his heart add to his lips, amounting to a reinforcement of the same thing (v. 23)?

_____

7. Pleasant words are described as what, going down to the soul and down to the bones (v. 24)?

_____

Notice that wisdom in this passage goes from the inside to the outside, and then it travels from the outside back down to the bones of others.

Beware of verbal scribbling. Edifying conversations require discipline and thought, and words should be weighed more than counted.

8. Look up Proverbs 15:28. What does the heart of the righteous do with regard to words?

_____

9. This is in contrast to the mouth of the wicked, which does what?

_____

Now the point of this chapter is not all the bad things you will do if you pour out evil things (although you will). Rather, the point of the comparison is to think of the positive good you will do if you study "how to answer." The point of thinking about one's answers is not simply in order to "stay out of trouble."

10. What is the point of conversation in Ephesians 4:29?

_____

The point is to do what is pleasant, good, and righteous, *and to do it with words.*

Suppose some parents said to a child something like this: "Now, while we are gone, we don't want you to spend any time on the trampoline. Instead we want you work on your reading for school." Suppose further the parents came home later to discover a child who had done no reading, but who had *not* gone near the trampoline, and who therefore thought he had been obedient. Now what?

Earrings go in the ears, and not in the eyebrows. There is a place for everything, and everything in its place. It is the same with words. If you take a sapling, which is a good thing, and try to plant it in your sidewalk, you cannot defend the folly by insisting that saplings are a good thing.

11. In Proverbs 25:11–12, what is compared to jewelry in the right place?

_____

Someone who is only interested in venting his own heart does not need to consider the destination. In other words, in speaking, is the goal to dump or to fill?

12. In Proverbs 10:32, what do the lips of the righteous know?

_____

One of the dangers of abstraction is that we start imagining that sentences should be evaluated simply on the basis of truth, and so we neglect larger issues of contextual propriety.

13. In Proverbs 15:23, what is so good about a good word?

_____

14. Notice that everywhere the Scriptures link the tongue and the heart. What is the nature of the interesting comparison in Proverbs 10:20?

_____

And the Lord Jesus put the question past all dispute. "O generation of vipers, how can ye, being evil, speak good things? for *out of the abundance of the heart the mouth speaketh*. A good man out of the good treasure of the heart bringeth forth good things: and an evil man out of the evil treasure bringeth forth evil things. But I say unto you, That every idle word that men shall speak, they shall give account thereof in the day of judgment" (Mt. 12:34–36).

This is not a promise that in the judgment God will lose all sense of proportion, and begin straining out the gnats in your idle words. Rather, it is making the profound point that idle words are sufficient to determine the content of the heart. If I found a bottle of vinegar, one drop on the tongue would tell me what it was. And would this be unfair to the rest of the bottle?

So, do good with your words. Again, the issue is positive good. How many times the Bible tells us this!

15. In Proverbs 10:11, what is the mouth of a righteous man? But what covers the mouth of the wicked?

_____

16. And what is a wholesome tongue in Proverbs 15:4?

_____

DIFFICULT DIFFERENCES

What happens when we emphasize community, life together, fellowship, communion, what the New Testament calls *koinonia*? The response to this kind of emphasis is generally significant—showing that there is a real spiritual hunger for this kind of thing. But there is a hitch—other people are involved. Many years ago, the French philosopher Sartre wrote a famous play, *No Exit*, where it concluded with, "Hell is other people." But we are Christians, and so we are called to affirm, to the contrary, that *heaven* is other people. But a fallen world lies in between us and that heaven, and there are difficult relationships to deal with.

First look up Philippians 2:1–5, and answer the following questions. Paul is about to set before us the great example of Christ's servant-heart (vv. 6ff). This is an example that he wants us to follow, and he gives us the charge before the example comes.

1. If there is any consolation in Christ (v. 1), and there is, and if God provides any comfort of love, and He does, and if He creates fellowship in the Spirit, which He certainly does, if there is a deep empathetic connection in the gut between Christians, then what does Paul want them to do, right at the beginning of v. 2?

_____

2. How would we go about fulfilling Paul's joy? What is the first thing (v. 2)?

_____

3. And the second?

_____

4. The third?

_____

5. And the fourth?

_____

So we need to be like-minded, sharing the same love, being in agreement, and settled in one mind (v. 2).

6. In verse 3, what should we guard ourselves against?

_____

7. What will lowliness of mind do for others?

_____

8. What should we esteem in the first place (v. 3)?

_____

9. What should we not think on first (v. 4)?

_____

This is the kind of thing Jesus did, and so Paul then proceeds to talk about that stupendous example (vv. 5ff).

So let us spend some time thinking about factors to consider as we try to think about where the other person is? How can we go about this intelligently? There are three basic assumptions that cause conflict among Christians, factors that contribute to what we might call difficult relationships. First, we tend to assume that every disruption is the direct result of sin, pure and simple. Second, we assume that we know what that sin is. And third, we assume that it is the other person's sin. All three of these assumptions are drastically, radically wrong-headed.

We are commanded in this passage to strive toward certain things in common—like-mindedness, being of one mind, a shared fellowship in the Spirit, mutual giving, and so on.

This does not mean that we can only do this if we start from some clone-like identity. No, we serve and worship a triune God, who has built some glorious *differences* into the world. We are to proceed from those differences to the unity described, which is not the same thing as obliterating those differences for the sake of a unity *not* described. What are some of those differences that have to be embraced at the starting point? You are cooking with onions and eggs, not trying to turn onions into eggs.

Now, of course, some of the differences we have might be the result of sin, but just as often our sin is the result of not understanding our differences. Then when we sin, we just add bad cooking to the breakfast of eggs and onions.

Here are some of the glorious built-in differences, some of the onions.

Different personality types: do not dismiss this just because you have heard it described by some secular psychologist. Every observant person in the history of the world has known the differences between Pooh, Rabbit, Eeyore, and Tigger. Give them other names (e.g. choleric, melancholic, sanguine, and phlegmatic), or rearrange them and call them something else. Like the fact of gravity, it is something we all have to deal with and, also like gravity, this reality is equally stubborn.

Men and women: the differences between how men and women think, respond, emote, etc., are deep and profound. Men are linear; women think laterally. Men are goal-oriented; women are relationship-oriented. Men seek respect before love; women seek love before respect. Men want honor; women want security. Men want solutions; women want conversation. What a world we live in!

Culture and race: there are deep differences between a hardscrabble Scot, an expressive Greek, and an inscrutable Japanese. Our PC world should deal with it.

Age and birth order: how can someone who is sixty years old still be the little sister? And still feel like she has to compete for Dad's attention?

Mix and match: now take the categories outlined above, and see how many other different combinations you can get. Outgoing African woman; shy, retiring, introspective Asian-American man. You get the picture.

Now if you tend to think that every "head bonk" is the result of sin, you are going to wind up thinking that the whole world is engaged in a vast, perverse conspiracy, designed and operated solely in order to offend you grievously every day, all day long.

The passage we considered above said that we are to esteem others better than ourselves. We tend to judge others by their actions, and ourselves by our motives. And since this collision "must be" the result of sin, we immediately try to diagnose what sin it is. And naturally, we always lift the hood of the other guy's car first. We always give ourselves the advantage. But Paul says here to give the advantage, the benefit of the doubt, the other way.

Ignoring the creational distinctives that God has given us is a good way to get "one up" on everybody. If you had done *that*, then your motives would have been *thus and such*. They did that, and so their motives must have been what yours would have been. This is a recipe for one conflict after another. Those who resort to this tactic frequently accuse others of sin, but they are the ones bringing the sin to the situation. We are so focused on identifying what his sin *must* be, that we neglect entirely what our sin *might* be. When Paul says to avoid strife and vainglory, he says that we are, in lowliness of *mind*, to consider the possibility that the person with the other perspective *has a point*. Yes, but—you want to scream—you have a point too, and nobody's listening! Well, let go of it, and maybe they will. Put it *down* for a second.

The apostle knows that striving for this kind of like-mindedness is not a day at the beach (4:2), but it most necessary. To return to the cooking metaphor, we are not trying to make a simple bowl of Cream of Wheat, without the sugar. We are making a complicated dish, with hundreds of ingredients, and when we are done we want to still be able to taste both the rum *and* the coconut. This is Trinitarian community, Trinitarian *koinonia*.

STRANGE CONTENTMENT

Someone once said that if you keep your head when all around you people are losing theirs, then you obviously don't understand the situation. The joke works because we know what we tend to do. Rightly understood, contentment is impossible to understand. A book which sets itself to *explain* it is therefore heading into treacherous waters. We need to be careful to explain only those aspects of it that are laid out in the Word, and then leave the Holy Spirit to His work in bringing about contentment in our lives.

1. Let's start by looking up Philippians 4:6–7. According to this passage, what should make us anxious?

_____

2. As we avoid anxiety, how many things should we pray about?

_____

3. What should always be included in such prayer?

_____

4. As we make our requests to God, what will happen?

_____

5. Does this make sense to us?

_____

6. Now look up Colossians 3:15. What should rule in our hearts?

_____

7. What were we called to in one body?

_____

8. And what should we be in addition?

_____

So when it comes to contentment, it is so easy for us to slip off the point, and so we should take special care to look directly at what these passages are saying. We should do so expecting to be surprised. If God is going to do something in our lives that passes all understanding, we should perhaps expect the run-up to contain something of the unexpected also. In the Colossians passage, we have the duty of contentment stated. But notice how it is stated. The peace of God is to be sovereign. Let the peace of God _rule_, he says. Notice also that contentment is a corporate duty—we are called to this, he says, "in one body." God's intent with regard to contentment is that it be manifested in a corporate way, within the body. And third, notice the close association of contentment with thanksgiving and gratitude.

In Philippians, we also have the duty stated—be careful or anxious for nothing. We then move into what we think is familiar territory. The apostle tells us to pray. This is something we know to do, but we frequently don't do it the way we are instructed here. We do let our requests be known to God, and we do this by means of prayer and supplication. But this leads to the very common problem of worrying on our knees. We pray and we pray and we pray, like Sisyphus pushing his rock up that hill in Hades. We never get to closure. We try to get the issue shut, but the latch never _clicks_. Just because worrying on our knees looks "spiritual" doesn't make it fun.

9. So what is the armor that protects us?

_____

Our tendency—when we are worrying on our knees—is to try to figure out a way for our hearts and minds to guard the peace of God. We consider contentment, the peace of God, to be our soft innards which must be protected by the hard shield of our works, plans, thoughts, understanding, and so on. We try to protect the wrong thing with the wrong thing. But the peace of God guards your hearts and minds; your hearts and minds do not protect the peace of God. The peace of God is armor. It is no fragile thing. The peace of God is not a guttering candle in a tornado, certain to go out. The thing that mystifies us about this is how _strong_ the peace of God is. And one thing is sure: we are told here that the peace of God guards us, and we do not guard it.

Knowing this, we offer our prayers with thanksgiving. But thanksgiving takes a very different form than presenting a raw petition alone. Thanksgiving is different than a straight request. Thanksgiving offered in faith is still gratitude. It is still *thanks*. "I thank You, Father . . ."

This is something the Lord Jesus Himself did. We know that He presented His petition in the Garden of Gethsemane, and He did so with loud cries. He agonized over the petitions He was presenting. He knew what going to the cross would involve. And yet, what was the context of His request? Earlier, when He had taken the bread at the Supper, He said that it was His broken body, and He *gave thanks*. He was obviously giving thanks by faith—He was not giving thanks as part of an emotional rush. The cross was still in front of Him. He gave thanks over His own broken body before the prayer in the garden. Scripture tells us that for the joy that was set before Him He endured the cross, despising the shame. So thanksgiving can be spontaneous and unforced when the object of your desire is realized. But thanksgiving can also be rendered by faith before the natural and emotional thanksgiving arrives for the celebration.

So let's put all this together. You have a trouble, a discontent. It may be unwarranted, or there may be real reasons, genuine troubles. In the Lord's case, He was dealing with a real trial. We face real trials as well, and nothing said here about contentment should be seen as minimizing such trials. You may have a loved one who is dying. You may have hostile persecution at work. You may be facing financial disaster, and not of your making. In all this, we should remember that a servant is not greater than his master. If the Lord Jesus could give thanks at the beginning of His trial—and there has never been any other trial like it—then we can give thanks at the beginning of our trials. It can be a bit of work understanding how this armor goes on, but once on, the peace of God which protects your hearts and minds passes understanding. Others around you cannot understand how your heart and mind are withstanding the blows. They see the blows, and they see your response. They don't see the armor.

But other times—unfortunately, many other times—our discontent is simply a matter of murmuring or grumbling. We do our best to imitate the children of Israel in the wilderness. Too hot, too cold, too wet, too dry, too much, too little, and all topped off with a *poor me*. In these circumstances, presenting our petitions to God, with thanksgiving, amounts to confession of sin, and our discontent just vanishes like the attitude problem it was.

So be honest to God. We come before the Lord with an anxiety, a worry. We have trouble, and it troubles us. We lay it out before God, like Hezekiah in the temple. We present the difficulty, and we do not put three layers of holyspeak varnish on it. In other words, we are not required to pretend that we are not troubled when we actually are. We are not required to pretend that our troubles are not troubles. Look at the psalmist. These psalms are in our Bibles for very good reasons, and one of those reasons is to teach us how to pray. When it comes to his troubles, the inspired psalmist is frequently a noisy bucket. Presenting our petitions and requests to God should be an honest activity. Let it all out.

But here is the strange part. St. Paul tells us to do this, but he also adds that we are to do it with thanksgiving. Keep a psalter or a hymnal available. When you have laid all your troubles before the Lord, pick out a psalm of thanksgiving and sing it. This is the pattern: present, thank, rest. Remember, it is not your job to protect the peace of God. His peace is there to protect you.

LIVING IN THE WILL OF GOD

What Christian does not want to live in the will of God? What an admirable aspiration, and what a difficult thing to figure out. Many Christians have needlessly tied themselves up in knots over this issue.

1. Look up James 4:13–17. Who is James addressing?

_____

2. What is the problem with their plans?

_____

3. What is their life actually like?

_____

4. What should they say instead of what they have been saying?

_____

5. What are they rejoicing in?

_____

6. What is the problem with it?

_____

7. How does James define sin here?

_____

James is addressing professing Christians who are in the middle of making business plans, and he insists that they do so while taking the will of God into account. But note what he does not say. He does not say that "you should first prayerfully determine that it is in fact God's will." He says rather that you need to hold your plans before Him with open palms, because you do not know what the will of God is. He is addressing those who are in the midst of plans (v. 13). He responds to this, not with an exhortation to pietistic assurance, but rather to the kind of humility that comes from internalizing the book of Ecclesiastes. Your life, and mine, is a *vapor* (v. 14). This means that all our plans should be made contingently—*if* the Lord wills, we will do this or that (v. 15). If you do not live this way, the simplest statement becomes a boastful evil (v. 16). If you have been taught this principle, to refuse to do it is an overt sin (v. 17).

We have to resist the sin of high presumption. The sin that James identifies here is that of saying, "I am going to do thus and such," when your life is a mist, and you can't know that. Now, suppose a man desperately wants to live in the will of God, and wants to do nothing unless it is the will of God. He prays all night, and tells his friends that he wants to move forward on this business venture, and God will surely bless it, "because I am confident that it is the will of God." Is his life still a mist and a vapor? *Yes.* Has he received a special revelation from God? Is he a prophet? *No.* Then this means that his pietism has driven him a great deal further into the sin that James is condemning, which is the sin of presumption. Presumption doesn't cease to be presumption because you bring in the name of God and pretend to know His unrevealed will. This merely heightens the presumption that James already condemned as *evil.*

There is another important distinction that we have to master when considering this subject. If we don't, we will find ourselves all tangled up because we have not carefully distinguished what we mean by "the will of God." The phrase can refer, with equal appropriateness, to the decrees of God, or to the commands of God. We can and should use the phrase both ways, but if we think we are talking about one when we are talking about the other, the result will be practical mayhem. The decrees of God are the will of God for how every detail of human history plays out. This is basic.

8. How many things does God work out (Eph. 1:11)?

_____

9. What does God's will include (Mt. 10:29)?

_____

10. Was the death of Jesus a tragic mistake (Acts 4:27–28)?

_____

Now Jesus, when He prayed about what these men were going to do to Him, spoke of it as *the will* of the Father (Lk. 22:42). Used in this sense the will of God *cannot be thwarted*. So if that were the only sense, then it wouldn't make any sense to try to live "in the will of God." In this sense, you can't get out of the will of God.

But there is another use of the phrase in Scripture, and in this sense the will of God is thwarted all the time. Is it the will of God for us to refrain from adultery? Of course. Do all Christians refrain from it? Unfortunately, no.

11. Look up 1 Thessalonians 4:1–3. What is described as the will of God there?

_____

12. Is it the kind of "will of God" that can be thwarted?

_____

This is the preceptive will of God (referring to His precepts), which can be thwarted, and frequently is. So then, distinguish the decrees (which are hidden from us beforehand—our lives are a vapor) and the commands, which belong to us and our children (Deut. 29:29).

So then, how do we go about making an actual decision? We are not supposed to try to figure out the (decretive) will of God beforehand, getting a preprinted agenda from the Holy Spirit, so that we can go off and do it. But we are still responsible to walk in the will of God, honoring Him. But how can we do this without figuring it all out beforehand? In this sense, there are two elements to living in the will of God—obedience and wisdom.

First, obedience. You never have to pray about whether to marry an unbeliever. You never have to pray about whether to violate a lawful contract you made. You never have to pray about whether to break a lawful promise to someone. God's Word, God's preceptive will, given to all Christians, directs you.

What about wisdom? Assuming the choice before you is lawful—the job offer is not to become a hit man for the Mafia or a hooker—what do you do then? You seek the wisdom of parents, family, friends, and counselors as you seek to answer the following three questions: What are your *abilities*? What are your *opportunities*? What are your *desires*? "Where no counsel is, the people fall: but in the multitude of counsellors there is safety" (Prov. 11:14).

Abilities: "For I say, through the grace given unto me, to every man that is among you, not to think of himself more highly than he ought to think; but to think soberly, according as God hath dealt to every man the measure of faith" (Rom. 12:3).

Opportunities: "Withal praying also for us, that God would open unto us a door of utterance…" (Col. 4:3).

Desires: "Delight thyself also in the LORD; and he shall give thee the desires of thine heart" (Ps. 37:4).

We should labor to make what we understand to be important decisions in this careful way. But we must never believe that everything rides on us. We do this because God is growing us up into maturity, and not because we have a clear list of which decisions before us are crucial and which are unimportant. *We* don't know. Never forget that God is God, and we live our lives trusting in Him.

CHRIST HIDDEN IN YOUR CALLING

Now on the subject of work, we must first begin with a statement of our problem. Many glorious truths were recovered in the Reformation, and one of them was the doctrine of vocation. Unfortunately, this is part of our Protestant heritage that we have shamefully neglected, and have almost lost. One of the principal indications that we have lost this doctrine is that we speak easily and readily of "full-time Christian work," as though there were anything else for a Christian to do. The reestablishment of two "holiness" layers of occupations in Christendom is a terrible loss.

1. Look up Exodus 31:1–5. Who did the Lord call in this passage?

_____

2. And what was he filled with?

_____

3. What four things resulted?

_____

4. What was he able to do?

_____

So the word of the Lord came to Moses (v. 1). A particular man was *called* by name out of the tribe of Judah. His name was Bezaleel (v. 2), and the Lord filled him with the Spirit of God (v. 3). This is the first instance of anyone being described as filled with the Spirit in the Bible. And what were the indications of the Spirit's filling? They were wisdom, understanding, knowledge, and craftsmanship (v. 3), which gave him the ability to do cunning work—as a goldsmith, a silversmith, a worker in brass (v. 4), as a jeweler (or possibly a mason), a woodworker, along with any other similar work.

So when the Spirit descends to fill a man for the first time in the Bible, it is surprisingly not to come down upon a theologian reading a big, fat scroll. He does do that, but *later*. Now the important thing here is that Bezaleel was called. The Latin verb that means "to call" is *vocare*, from which we get our word "vocation," *calling*. This is not to disparage the importance of a call to the mission field, or the ministry—of course not. But *all* Christians are called, and are called to labor self-consciously and faithfully in their calling, whether it is law, real estate, carpentry, medicine, brick-laying, shop-keeping, changing diapers, writing novels or songs, digging latrines, or planting trees. All of God is in all of it.

We must therefore fix it in our minds that God is in everything, and works through everything. This means that Christ is hidden in the artisan, and Christ is hidden in the customer. Christ is hidden in the one behind the counter, and He is hidden in the one in front of the counter. He is hidden in the dentist, and hidden in the patient in the chair.

First, God provides *for* us through means. We benefit from the work of the farmer, the fertilizer salesman, the trucker, the grocery store clerk, the dairyman, and when we bow our heads to thank God for the breakfast cereal, we are thanking Him for His work *in all of these people*, whether they know Him or not. We receive from God through the work of others. We acknowledge this when we pray for our daily bread (Mt. 6:11). We know that God is working in and through all things (Rom. 8:28), and this includes countless daily kindnesses.

Second, Christ receives *from* us as we work in each of our vocations. God gratefully *receives* from us through the work we do for others. "Lord, when did I ever give you hot French fries when you were famished?" "Don't you remember? It was that time at the drive-through window." This is the other side of vocation. God keeps track of every cup of cold water (Mt. 10:42), and He reckons *everything* we do for others as done to Him (Mt. 25:34–46).

This means that Christ is hidden in our vocation, and He is hidden in our neighbor. We are to discover Him there with the eye of faith.

5. What were we created for? What does Genesis 2:15 say?

_____

6. How many days should we work (Exod. 20:9–11)?

_____

7. When we work, who should we remember is watching (Col. 2:23)?

_____

8. When we receive the fruit of any work done for us, who should we receive it as a gift from (Mt. 6:11)?

_____

The mother gives milk to the child, but who fills her breasts with milk in the first place? When the farmer first planted the wheat, he did not know he was making milk for the baby.

But we also have to consider what vocation does not mean. All work is full of glory, but it is a glory apprehended by faith. This faith does not necessarily mean that a Christian carpenter pounds nails differently than an unregenerate carpenter. But it *does* mean that he should understand the meaning of what he does, and, over time, this should result in differences in craft competence.

Neither should this doctrine be taken as an excuse to become a one-trick pony. Your vocation is varied, and extends to every aspect of your life. This means that you are not only called to be, say, a software designer, but you are also called to be a son, a student, a husband, a brother, a citizen, a churchman, and a putter of model ships into bottles. Incidentally, parents, this means that education should be equipping your child for his or her vocation in this *broad* sense, not the narrow sense. And this, incidentally, is the meaning of a liberal arts education.

Vocation is not a talisman against worldly difficulties. Americans love "three steps to automatic success," but that is not what the Scriptures promise. Diligence in this way of thinking will *generally* result in long-term satisfaction with what you do—instead of the constant flitting from job to job that is so common in our day—but don't think that God-given changes are a sign that something is necessarily wrong. And don't think that vocation means that you will just float through your work day—the diapers can really stink, the customers can really be unreasonably irate, the promised shipments really can be subject to exasperating delays. Rain falls on the just and the unjust (Mt. 5:45). And Christ is in all of it.

Remember the earlier chapter on living in the will of God: what is His revealed will for all Christians, and, after that, what are your abilities, your opportunities, and your desires? When all that lines up, then go for it. "A man's heart deviseth his way: but the Lord directeth his steps" (Prov. 16:9). And as you go, remember this: "Seest thou a man diligent in his business? he shall stand before kings; he shall not stand before mean men" (Prov. 22:29). This is not carnal ambition—it is what enables us to see *death and resurrection* in our daily callings.

Any attempt to address this subject would be grossly deficient if we did not quote Luther at some point. His wonderful grasp of vocation, the most heavenly and *earthy* of truths, was remarkable. "God Himself milks the cows through the vocation of the milkmaid." And amen.

DESIRE RUNS DEEP

One of our central duties—as Christians seeking to live obediently in this fallen world—is to learn the true nature of the temptations before us. The oldest trap in the world for us is to "objectify" sin in a simplistic way, placing certain items on a list of prohibitions, as though it would be so simple. And so we are going to take several chapters to consider the following four subjects—desire, envy, competition, and ambition.

1. First, look up Matthew 20:1–16. At the end of this story, why did the workers murmur against their employer?

_____

2. What did he say in reply?

_____

3. What inversion sums the whole thing up?

_____

We have here in this text an economic illustration of a spiritual and covenantal truth. The point of the parable is the relationship of Jews to Gentiles, the Jews having labored in the vineyard of the Lord for centuries, with the Gentiles breezing in at the last minute for some really good wages. At the same time, this kind of human reaction is a very common one, and it represents the kind of desire we are going to be considering.

We respond this way with covenantal privileges, with wages for work, with bowls of ice cream and more. The kingdom is like a householder who went out to hire workers for his vineyard (v. 1). He hires some to work all day for an agreed-upon price (v. 2). At the third hour, he hired some more without an agreed upon price (vv. 3–4). At the sixth and ninth hours, he did the same thing again (v. 5). At the eleventh hour, near the end of the day, he did the same thing *again* (vv. 6–7). When the day was over, the householder told his steward to pay everyone, starting with the last ones hired (v. 8). When this group was paid, they got what had been promised to the first group hired (v. 9). So when the first group got up to the pay table, they were naturally expecting more, but they got the exact terms of their contract instead (v. 10). Being sinners, they thought this was an injustice and grumbled about it (v. 11), saying that the householder had made the unequal equal (v. 12). The householder defended himself; justice was done (v. 13), and grace was extended (v. 14). What is it to you that I am being gracious to another (v. 15)? The last will be first, and the first last (v. 16).

We have not only rejected this biblical way of thinking, we have also as a culture reversed all the values (Is. 5:20). We have institutionalized our sin—if a farmer today tried this stunt, he would immediately be slapped with a class-action lawsuit. Not only so, but he would be accused of *injustice,* when his actions had been preeminently *just.* And if he took the stand in his own defense, and repeated the Lord's argument to the plaintiffs—"Take what is yours and go your way"—he would quickly discover that we don't like how Jesus thought and taught. We don't like it at the macro level (covenant history) and we don't like it at the micro level (different rates paid to kids for mowing your lawn). But *why* don't we like it? In order to answer the question, we have to distinguish between two different kinds of desire.

The first kind of desire is a creational, biological given. It is not social or corporate. You desire to breathe, for example. In the middle of a desert, you would want a drink of water, even if, especially if, the nearest town was a hundred miles away. An itch exactly halfway between your shoulder blades creates a desire that has nothing to do with anybody else. Let us call this simple desire, and let us thank God for it.

4. Look up Genesis 2:9. Why would anybody want to eat the fruit that God made available?

_____

No sin anywhere, and a world full of things to desire. God is good, and the created world is good to want, provided we know how to want it.

But we don't. Sin entered the world at the Fall, and right along with it, a completely different kind of desire. This kind of desire shapes far more of your life than you probably recognize. This kind of desire is the driving engine of our text. We can see it appear just a few pages into our Bibles: "And Cain was very wroth, and his countenance fell" (Gen. 4:5). This is the seed bed of envy, but we are not to envy yet. "Do ye think that the scripture saith in vain, The spirit that dwelleth in us lusteth to envy? But he giveth more grace" (Jas. 4:5–6).

So this second kind of desire runs far deeper than you probably recognize. Trying to see it is like trying to see the air we breathe. Trying to see it is like trying to see your own eyeball. This kind of desire is the kind of thing we use to look *with,* instead of learning how (by the grace of God) to look *at* it. This kind of desire— interwoven desire, metaphysical desire—is not something we tend to bring to the bar of God's justice; rather, we use it idolatrously *as the* bar of justice. We want, and therefore we know what all others should want on our behalf (if only they had a sense of "justice").

Step out of your desires for a moment. Learn to look at your life as though you were watching a movie, and "you" were a character up on the screen there. View your wants dispassionately, with a sense of justice that is not fed by the simple fact of your desiring. This is the heart of what Jesus provided for us in the *profound* ethic of the Golden Rule. "Therefore all things whatsoever ye would that men should do to you, do ye even so to them: for this is the law and the prophets" (Mt. 7:12). Note what obedience to this requires—it *requires* you to step out of yourself. The Golden Rule is *not* a fancy way of telling you to "be nice." Nice people are often vicious when their niceness is not appropriately recognized. The Lord's words require you to treat your desires as authoritative, but not authoritative in the treatment others give to *you*.

If you are "caught up" in this kind of desire, this means that you are wanting things because others want them, or because others have them, or because you believe that others want them, or you believe that others have them. Moreover, when you are caught up this way, there is no *reasoning* with you. And when God gives "more grace," it is this problem that He is giving the grace to address. What are the sorts of things that we desire when we are desiring wrongly this way? Our desires include, but are not limited to: the favor and blessing of God, the birth status of your older brother, her looks, his wife's looks, her education, his height, her body, his paycheck, his self-confidence . . . him being hired for easy money at the eleventh hour. If desire is authoritative in the mere fact of wanting, such irrational desires don't seem irrational to the person in the grip of them. And this is why desire of this kind must be addressed by *grace*, and not by a logical argument.

HEAVIER THAN WET SAND

In this section, we are considering the temptations presented to us by desire, envy, competition, and ambition. In the previous chapter we looked at *desire*—the quarry from which many sins are hewn—a word which, thankfully for the writers of rock ballads, rhymes with *fire*. We now turn to the thing that our spirits' desires naturally run to, which is *envy*.

1. Let's start with James 4:1–3. In a rhetorical question in the first verse, James wants to know the origins of what?

_____

2. In the second verse, what does the intense desire of "lust" lead to?

_____

3. Why is the request refused when we ask God for it?

_____

4. Now read James 4:4–6. It is not possible to be friends with two things at the same time. What are those two things?

_____

5. What does the Bible say about the spirit that dwells in us?

_____

6. What does God give us in response to this tendency we have to veer off toward envy?

_____

7. Who does God fight? Who does He help?

_____

Consider what the writer of Proverbs teaches.

"A stone is heavy, and the sand weighty; but the fool's wrath is heavier than them both. Wrath is cruel, and anger is outrageous; but who is able to stand before envy?" (Prov. 27:3–4).

The writer of Proverbs begins with an illustration. A heavy stone is hard to pick up (v. 3), and the same thing is true of sand (v. 3). And when a fool gets angry, that is heavier than both or either of them. You should rather have your pickup filled with wet sand than to encounter an angry fool. Then, building on that first thought, since we are now at the next level, wrath is cruel (v. 4). The synonym *anger* is outrageous (v. 4), but envy carries everything before it. Envy is therefore a *formidable* sin.

As we attempt to sort this out, let us begin with definitions. Jealousy is to be possessive of what is lawfully your own. Because we are sinners, we sometimes give way to jealousy for wrong causes, or in a wrong manner, but Scripture is clear that jealousy is not inherently sinful. Our God is a jealous God; His *name* is Jealous (Exod. 20:5; 34:14).

Simple greed or covetousness wants what it does not have, and wants to have it without reference to God's conditions for having it. The thing that it wants may have been seen in a store, a catalog, or a neighbor's driveway. This sin is tantamount to idolatry (Eph. 5:5), putting a created thing in place of the Creator.

But envy is more than excessive jealousy, and is far more than simply a lazy or idolatrous desire. Envy is a formidable sin, as the text above shows, because it combines its own desires for the object (status, money, women, whatever) with a malicious insistence that the other person *lose* his possession of it.

In two places Paul puts malice and envy cheek by jowl (Rom. 1:28–29; Tit. 3:3), and this is no accident. In the Bible, when envy moves, violence and coercion are not far off (Acts 7:9; 13:45; 17:5; Mt. 27:18). Envy sharpens its teeth every night. We may therefore define envy as a particular kind of willingness to use coercion to deprive someone of what is lawfully his.

Now this is the natural condition of man. We saw earlier that the spirit within us "lusteth to envy" (Jas. 4:5–6). This is our natural tendency; it is a universal problem. We saw also that a recognition of complicity in the sin is the way of escape. That recognition is called repentance, and can only be found in Christ.

8. Outside of Christ, envy is the natural condition of all mankind. Before we were converted, what were we like? Look up Titus 3:3, and write down what environment nonbelievers dwell in.

_____

9. *That* is what we are like. Now look up Romans 1:29. Name three of envy's companions.

_____

When we are brought into Christ, this does not grant us automatic immunity to this sin—we must still guard ourselves. We have to reckon ourselves dead to sin and alive to God, and that includes death to this sin. For example, the godly have to be told not to envy sinners (Prov. 3:29–32; 23:17–18). And we have to guard ourselves against sanctimonious envy, the kind Judas tried to display in his false concern for the poor (Mk. 14:5, 10; Jn. 12:3–6).

This is an invisible vice. In striking contrast to many other sins, nobody readily admits to being envious. Envy is petty and malicious. Envy is unattractive to just about everybody, and in order to operate openly in the world, it has to sail under false colors. Envy is clandestine; envy is sneaky. To admit to envy is to admit self-consciously to being tiny-souled, beef jerky-hearted, petty, and mean-spirited, and to *admit* this is dangerously close to repentance. To be out-and-out envious is to be clearly in the wrong.

Envy often decks itself out with the feathers of admiration, and tends to praise too loudly or too much. One writer said to "watch the eyes of those who bow lowest." The praise can come from someone who does not yet know his own heart, or it can come from someone who is trying to position himself to get within striking distance. Guard your heart; don't become a Uriah Heep.

Envy occupies itself much with matters of justice, and becomes a collector of injustices, both real and imagined. Since envy cannot speak its own name, the closest virtue capable of camouflaging the sin is zeal for justice. And since true Christians should be very much concerned with true justice, be sure to run diagnostics on your heart as you do so.

Envy gets worse as the gifts get greater—when dealing with talent, artistic temperaments, and great intellectual achievements. We sometimes assume that we can "cultivate" our way out of the temptation, which is the reverse of the truth.

Because we are naive about this sin, in ourselves and in others, we glibly assume that if God only blesses us a little bit more, that will make it clear that we are nice people and that there is no reason to envy us. But of course, this only makes everything worse. Should the "neighbor" in the tenth commandment assume that if God only gave him a bigger house and faster car that this would somehow resolve the problems of his green-eyed neighbor next door? Is he serious?

You are at the beginning of your lives, your careers, your accomplishments. And you need to know that when marked success comes to some of you, the poison will start to flow. Even in the church? Yes, even here, but if we take note of our hearts now, if we internalize these truths now, we are laboring for the peace and purity of our congregation—one of the things we are covenanted to in our membership vows. When James takes aim at conflict in the church, he takes aim at envy. So remember that the love of Christ is forever, and envy is transient. Speaking of the earthbound, Solomon says, "Also their love, and their hatred, *and their envy, is now perished*; neither have they any more a portion for ever in any thing that is done under the sun" (Eccl. 9:5–6).

Gore Vidal once said, "Whenever a friend succeeds, a little something in me dies." In stark contrast, the apostle Paul said, "Love does not envy" (1 Cor. 13:4).

COMPETITION

We are continuing to consider the problems posed by desire, envy, competition, and ambition. We have now come to competition, something dear to the heart of most Americans. But because of this we must guard our step. You have heard many times that we must repent of our virtues, and this subject is a good place to start.

1. Look up Philippians 2:3–4. No action should have the following two characteristics. What are they?

_____

2. What does lowliness of mind do for others?

_____

3. Each person should not look out for what?

_____

4. Instead of this, what should each person look out for?

_____

Now this passage is taken from the chapter in which the perfect humility of Christ was exalted to the highest place. This is not presented to us as a striking anomaly, but rather as being central to what we as Christians are called to imitate. How many things are we allowed to do because of our striving (v. 3)? Nothing. How about vainglory (v. 3)? Nothing again. What should our mindset be toward others? St. Paul replies we should consider them "better," that is, more important than we do ourselves. This is to be our central disposition. This is to be characteristic of how our mind goes. Paul then says that we are not to look on our own things (v. 4), but *also* on the things of others (v. 4). This word in the second half of the phrase helps us to understand what is meant in the first half. This is a comparative statement, not an absolute statement. It is similar to when Paul tells each of us to carry our own burden (Gal.

6:5), carry our own weight. This is fully consistent with his exhortation for us to carry one another's burdens (Gal. 6:2). *Only the mind of Christ can sort this out.*

5. If you are an accomplished pianist, and somebody else couldn't find middle C if you let them use both hands, does the first guy have to pretend that the second guy is a "better" pianist than he is? What does Paul mean here by better?

_____

Now, if we have a competitive system, is it every man for himself, and devil take the hindmost? There is a *laissez-faire* approach to competition that is very important for the civil magistrate to remember when it comes to the question of him restricting, regulating, organizing, or otherwise botching economic activity. But, as you have been reminded many times, there is a difference between sins and crimes. And just because something ought not to be criminal, with penalties attached, does not mean that it is healthy and automatically non-sinful. Lust ought not to be against the law, but that doesn't make it okay. The civil magistrate is not competent to outlaw greed either, and all messianic attempts to do so have been disastrous. However . . .

There are Christians who see this, and who conclude from it that a "let 'er rip" attitude should be allowed everywhere. But the civil magistrate is not prohibited from addressing greed because it is an invisible sin. It is *not* invisible, and other governments are required to deal with it. For example, a family can see and identify what their problem is.

6. Look up Proverbs 15:27. What does a greedy person do there?

_____

7. Now look up 1 Tim. 3:3 and 3:8. What is the church required to do there?

_____

8. And should this issue be taken into account when we go to vote in civic elections (Exod. 18:21)?

_____

The Bible requires us not to elect officials unless they hate covetousness. We have taken this to mean that we shouldn't vote for them unless they are *steeped* in it. Our political parties taken together constitute a Society for the Prevention of Cruelty to Money. But this is not right.

Now the fact that even a good civil government is not competent to outlaw greed does not mean that no entity is competent to deal with it. The family and church must deal with it. And voters in civic elections should deal with it.

In our text, the word "better" is a rendering of *hyperecho*. What does lowliness of mind require of us in this? Remember we are trying to build the mind of Christ, which cannot be done out of two-by-fours. We tend to read the English here as requiring us to believe that the other person is better at doing whatever it is we might be comparing, which is obviously crazy. Having run into this superficial roadblock, we dismiss the entire problem from our minds. But this is dangerous. The word *hyperecho* can also be rendered as "to be above, to stand out." That does not make the other person automatically right, or superior in his abilities. Remember that the one we are imitating in this is the Lord Jesus—when He became a man, He did so because He believed we were "better" (in this sense) than He was. This obviously has to mean the sense of "more important, more valued." Jesus did not die for us because we were better than He in some moral sense. He died for us because He *loved* us more than He loved His own life. So the issue is humility and love, and nothing in this requires us to embrace absurdities.

Now our task is to learn how to bear our own burden (providing for our own family, meeting our own responsibilities) at the same time we are careful to bear one another's burdens (holding to a true fellowship of goods). The early Christians kept their own property (Acts 5:4), *and* they held all things in common (Acts 4:32–33). Here are a few basic principles as we pursue the mind of Christ, as we long for "great grace to be upon us all."

9. How do we know that the early Christians continued to hold property (Acts 5:4)?

_____

10. How do we know that they shared (Acts 4:32–33)?

_____

Now, you are learning how to compete here and now—in your athletics, in your grades, and so on. You are going out into a world where the competition is intense, and this means that you have to learn how to do it. We have already discussed desire and envy, which run down the middle of *every* human heart. Deal with all the big problems there first. And don't think that thirty seconds of reflection or mere intellectual assent is going to do the trick.

Secondly, learn how justice fits into grace. Don't go the other way, trying to fit grace into justice. Grace corrodes when stored in justice. Justices thrives and grows strong in grace. It is better to be taken to the cleaners because you loaned money, expecting nothing back (Lk. 6:35) than to have an evil eye, tight fist, and wary heart (Mk. 7:22).

11. How many trees were prohibited in the Garden of Eden, and how many were allowed?

_____

Third, work hard and intelligently, expecting your work to not only provide for your responsibilities, but also to be a blessing to any brother who is "competing" for the same customers you are. That's impossible, you say. Tell it to God, who traffics in impossibilities. Zero-sum thinking is the logic of unbelief—where more for you means less for me.

This is how we must learn to live in a cut-throat world. Keeping ourselves free from strife and vainglory seems like an overwhelming task sometimes. What are we to do about the outside world, which does not appear to be functioning with this calculus at all? What grasping and ravenous entities are out there? Besides Microsoft, the U.S. government, assorted televangelists, the Republicrats, the United Nations, the Southern Poverty Law Center, and more? What should we do about all that? First, we must not envy them (Prov. 3:29–32; 23:17–18). Second, we must not imitate them or their ways (Mt. 20:25–26). And third, we should live in our communities such that we teach them a more excellent way (1 Cor. 12:31).

REAL AMBITION

So we have considered desire, envy, and competition, and we now come to ambition. To address the subject rightly, we have to recall what we learned thus far. There is a certain kind of desire that every human being has to deal with, and this is a desire that tends to veer toward envy. If God has not given us the grace of being able to see this in ourselves, we will come into competitive situations motivated in the wrong way entirely. And the same thing is true of our ambitions. Our ambitions will lust after what God has never given.

1. Look up Luke 14:7–11. Why did Jesus tell this parable? What did He notice?

_____

2. According to His teaching, what should we not do at a wedding?

_____

3. Why shouldn't we do this?

_____

4. If that were to happen, what would be the effect on us?

_____

5. So what approach should we take to the seats of honor?

_____

6. Is the lesson here to never sit in a seat of honor? If not, what is the lesson?

_____

7. What is the bottom-line principle that Jesus gives?

_____

Christ tells us a parable that reveals His shrewd humility. But at the same time, if we understand Him, we see it is a true humility—this kind of thing offered up to God as a "trick that He won't see through" is obviously crazy. This must be done *before God openly*. On one occasion Jesus saw a bunch of people jockeying for position somewhere, angling for that elusive place of honor (v. 7). He then told them a parable about the seating arrangements at a wedding, and He said not to take the seat of honor (v. 8). If you do, a more honorable guest will certainly show up, and the host will have to take you down a few notches, perhaps *all* the notches (v. 9). Voluntarily take the lowest place, He says, and you will be invited up—to the applause of all (v. 10). And having said all this, Christ gives the principle. The man who exalts himself will be taken down. The man who humbles himself will be exalted (v. 11). This is because God opposes the proud, but gives grace to the humble (Jas. 4:6). This is a principle that runs *throughout* the Lord's teaching, and throughout the Bible. "I tell you, this man went down to his house justified [rather] than the other: for every one that exalteth himself shall be abased; and he that humbleth himself shall be exalted" (Lk. 18:14).

Our culture has been profoundly shaped and affected by the Lord's teaching. This is the case even though numerous individuals don't have the heart of the matter within them. The obvious rightness of the Lord's requirement is nevertheless reflected in our customs and manners in a way that was not true in the ancient world. But all this means is that the subtlety of sin has to take an extra hairpin turn in its way up Pride Mountain. We now have folks taking the lowest place as the way of manipulating situations and looking humble to boot. But just *saying* the right thing (like the Pharisee in the temple) is not good enough. We don't want to be like the woman in the old blues song with "a handful of gimme, and a mouthful of thank you, honey."

We must not be confused about ambition. We need to know *what* the adversary is—because if we have been paying attention, we already know *where* the adversary is: in our own hearts. "But if ye have bitter envying *and strife* in your hearts, glory not, and lie not against the truth. This wisdom descendeth not from above, but [is] earthly, sensual, devilish. For where envying *and strife* [is], there [is] confusion and every evil work" (Jas. 3:14–16). The word rendered as *strife* here is a particular kind of strife—it is not the strife of two armies colliding, but rather the strife that results from *electioneering* or *campaigning*. *Positioning* would be another word for it. The NIV renders it well as *selfish ambition*; we might say *striving ambition*. Now, who is the running mate in this campaign? Two times James tells us—envy, bitter envy. If this is the condition of your heart, don't lie to yourself about it (v. 14). This ambition does not come from above, but is diabolical (v. 15). And where you have envy and *this* kind of ambition together, you have "confusion and every kind of evil work." Always. This striving, this ambition, comes from a love of honors, a love of glory (Mk. 12:38–40), which is coupled with a hatred of the road that God has required for all who would come to His kind of honor and glory. We don't like that road because it runs through a deep valley. It is perfectly all right to be ambitious to climb the high mountain on the other side of that deep valley.

The person who is ambitious like this is begging for the opposition of God. Confusion and every evil work will dog him. God does not just make positive promises ("if you humble yourself, you will be exalted"). He also makes negative promises also ("if you push yourself to the front, He will see to it that you are set back"). When the disciples on the road got into an argument over who was the greatest, He spoke to them this way: "And he sat down, and called the twelve, and saith unto them, If any man desire to be first, [the same] shall be last of all, and servant of all" (Mk. 9:35; cf. 10:42–44). There are two ways to take this, both healthy.

We do not live in a pyramid world—which is another way of saying that glory and honor are not zero-sum games, any more than anything else in God's plan is. If you think that only one can occupy the top spot, and that you want to be that one, this will result in confusion and every kind of evil work. But God has created a rich, textured, and organic world, with an almost infinite array of options for *godly* ambition. There are two things to recognize—the first is that God is the master composer, and *His* symphony is going to be glorious beyond all reckoning. The second, just as important for your joy, is to find out what instrument you have been assigned and stop staring greedily at the first violin. In his introduction to a discussion of spiritual gifts, Paul says, "For I say, through the grace given unto me, to every man that is among you, *not to think [of himself] more highly than he ought to think*; but to think soberly, according as God hath dealt to every man the measure of faith" (Rom. 12:3). Godly ambition does not mean that any Christian can be at the top of the pyramid (making faces at the archangel Michael), provided he just humbles himself enough. This is not the spiritual equivalent of "any child can grow up to be president," which is (incidentally) a lie. Godly ambition means that those who humble themselves in accordance with God's Word will find themselves blessed to the maximum capacity that *their* gifts and calling will allow. To want anything more than that is to take hold of the wrong kind of ambition. Drop it; it is your death.

Jesus does not teach us that there is a problem with wanting to be great in the kingdom (Mt. 5:19). On repeated occasions, He instructs how to strive for that. He tells us how live in such a way that God says, "Well done." If you don't want that "well done," then something is really wrong. But if you want the "well done," here is the thing—you have to *do it well*. And doing it well involves imitating the Lord Jesus, who certainly had more reasons to not "stoop" than we do.

THE MEANING OF MASCULINITY

If you want to grow up to be "masculine," it is important to have some idea of what that is. And if you want your future spouse to grow up to masculine, it is equally important to know. We need to ground our definitions of masculinity in the teaching of the Bible. So what *is* masculinity anyway? A simple answer is that manhood is what boyhood should be aiming at.

A Bible teacher named Bill Mouser has pointed out five clear aspects of masculinity throughout the Bible. We shouldn't try to make these five aspects watertight, separating them completely from one another, but nevertheless, these *are* distinctive features of the masculine identity.

Men are first created to exercise dominion in the earth; second, they are equipped to be husbandman, tilling the earth; third, they are built to be saviors, delivering from evil; fourth, they are expected to grow up into wisdom, becoming wise, becoming sages; and last, they are designed to reflect the image and glory of God. So let's call them *lords, husbandmen, saviors, sages,* and *glory-bearers*.

1. Look up Genesis 1:26–28. This passage contains what is called the cultural mandate. What pattern does God use to make man?

_____

2. Man was to have dominion over what?

_____

3. After the list of creatures is given, over which man has dominion, what is he then told to do?

_____

4. Now some might want to assume that this cultural mandate was negated by the fall of man into sin, but God repeats the mandate again after the flood. Look up that passage (Gen. 9:1). Are there any significant differences?

_____

Sin certainly affected whether we could fulfill this command from God, and whether we could do it well, but it did not remove the obligation placed on us by the command. But if it is ever to be fulfilled now, in a fallen world, then God must help us. And given how kind God is, this is just what we see. The mandate is given to us yet again in another form in the Great Commission.

5. Look up Matthew 28:18–20. What are we told to do there?

_____

In boys, we should call this aspect of masculinity the "tree fort" impetus. Boys want to conquer and subdue, and if the territory before them is the backyard, then that is what they want to conquer and subdue. The point of discipline with boys is to channel and direct their energy into an obedient response to the cultural mandate. It is not to squash that energy, destroying it or making it sullen. Boys therefore should be in training to become men who exercise dominion; they should be learning to be lords in the earth, which means they should learn to be *adventurous* and *visionary*.

The second aspect is that of becoming a husbandman. Men were created not just to discover new worlds, but also to make them flourish. The dominion mandate, taken by itself, would just get us some pirates or biker gangs. So this second aspect means that men are created to conquer and subdue, and after this, *to settle down.*

6. Look up Genesis 2:15. What did God give man to do?

_____

Man does not just build ships and rockets. He also uses these things to move where he has gone, and he lives off of what he plants there—gardens, families, towns. Boys therefore should be learning to be *patient, careful,* and *hard-working.*

The third aspect of masculinity is very important. Boys and men want to save and protect. The greatest example of this is, of course, the Lord Jesus.

7. What was the promise that God gave us in Genesis 3:14–15?

_____

The ancient serpent, this dragon, was the one who tempted our first parents into sin. God promised a curse on that serpent, and it is in that curse that we see the salvation of the world. This is why St. George and the dragon stories appeal to us. Men who follow Jesus Christ, *the* dragon-slayer, must themselves become lesser dragon-slayers. And this is why it is absolutely *essential* for boys to play with wooden swords and plastic guns. Boys have a deep need to have something to defend, something to represent in battle. We are not pacifists, and so to beat spears into pruning hooks too early will just leave you fighting dragons with a pruning hook. This is why boys must learn how to fight. They must learn to be *strong, sacrificial, courageous,* and *good.*

The next point is troublesome to some young men. Men must learn to be wise, to be sages. In the book of Proverbs, wisdom is portrayed as a great lady. Sons are told to listen to her. In the first part of Proverbs (1–9), wisdom is a *woman* who disciplines boys. If he listens to her when he is a boy, then when he has grown up to wisdom, he has become a sage. This is why boys must learn the masculinity of study and of learning. Don't fall for the trap of setting one aspect of masculinity against another—sports and study, say. If this happens, a boy who naturally prefers the outdoors can too easily dismiss time in the library as effeminate, or, even worse, come to look down on poetry. Boys must therefore learn to be *teachable, studious,* and *thoughtful.*

8. The last aspect is that men are to be glory-bearers. Look up 1 Corinthians 11:7. What is man described as being there?

_____

9. And what is woman described as being?

_____

The woman reflects the glory of God by reflecting the glory of man, whose glory she is. However much feminists and egalitarians don't like it, God did not make the world according to their desires.

10. Look up 1 Corinthians 11:3. What is the head of man there?

_____

11. What is the head of woman?

_____

12. Look up Ephesians 5:23–24. What is the relationship of husband to wife there?

_____

These distinctions are not made in the interests of winning a contest. Star differs from star in glory. The sun and the moon differ from one another. When the Bible assigns one kind of glory to man and another kind of glory to woman, our modern prejudices prevent us from seeing that they are different kinds and levels of *glory*.

G. K. Chesterton wrote a short poem entitled "Comparisons" that shows us the problem:

If I set the sun beside the moon,
And if I set the land beside the sea,
And if I set the town beside the country,
And if I set the man beside the woman,
I suppose some fool would talk about one being better.

So boys must be instructed on how to grow up into glory and how to fulfill their responsibility to be *representative, responsible,* and *holy*.

Putting everything together, we should have a decent grasp of what God created masculinity to be like. Boys should be aggressive and adventurous, as lords of the earth. They should be patient and hard-working because they are learning husbandry. We should want them to hate evil, and they should want to challenge evil to a duel. They need to be deliverers, or saviors. Boys should be eager to learn from the wise, and want to become wise themselves. And they should deeply desire to stand before God, with head uncovered. They are the image and glory of God.

THE MEANING OF FEMININITY

In the previous chapter, we discussed five aspects of masculinity. Not wanting to leave the girls out, let us do the same for them. Here is something of what the Scriptures teach on the nature of femininity. She is *mistress of the domain, helper/fulfiller, life-giver, wise woman,* and *glory of man*. These in turn answer to the aspects of masculinity we discussed earlier—recall that we called them *lords, husbandmen, saviors, sages,* and *glory-bearers*.

As with boys, what we are going to grow up into, we need to aim for. Young ladies are future women, and they need to know what they are preparing for.

1. Now look up 1 Timothy 5:14. In this passage the apostle Paul is giving counsel to younger women on what they are to do. What should they become, with regard to the home?

_____

2. The phrase in the AV that is rendered "guide the house" is just one word in the Greek. That word is *oikodespotes*. The word *oiko* means "house." Does the rest of the word remind you of anything?

_____

3. From what is described here, does it appear that a woman has true authority in her home?

_____

We already considered how the husband is the head of the wife, which means that he has true authority. But at the same time, he delegates authority to her, and she is the "executive" of the home. In a very real way, a husband is a guest in the home. This can be taken in an unhelpful way, obviously, but that's not the way *we* should take it. This means that young women need to learn confidence and authority in their appointed domain, and they need to learn it self-consciously. Young women should be *confident, competent,* and *intelligent*.

4. Now look up Genesis 2:18–20. What did God say was "not good"?

_____

5. What did God resolve to do about the problem?

_____

6. After God said that He would create a helper suitable for Adam, what did He create first?

_____

7. What did Adam do with all of them?

_____

8. And what did he *not* find as he was naming the animals?

_____

9. And what is woman described as being?

_____

10. Look up 1 Corinthians 11:9. What does it say there?

_____

11. In Ephesians 1:22–23, how is the relationship between Christ and the Church described?

_____

This means that the man fills the woman and the woman fills the man, just as Christ and the church fill one another. This means that a woman needs to learn to be a *completer*, a *helper*, and a *fulfiller*.

12. For the third aspect, look up Genesis 3:20. Why does Adam give his wife the name "Eve"?

_____

13. In Genesis 4:1–2, who are the first two children born to Adam and Eve?

_____

14. In Deuteronomy 14:21, what is the requirement there?

_____

15. Why would this mean that women should not serve as combat troops?

_____

Since only women can be mothers, this means that young women should learn to *care*, *nurture*, *comfort*, and *nourish*.

16. What is wisdom described as being in Proverbs 1:20?

_____

17. What does she do in Proverbs 9:1?

_____

When Scripture describes wisdom in Proverbs, the imagery is consistently feminine. This means that women should be *educated*, *thoughtful*, and *wise*.

18. Look up 1 Corinthians 11:7. What does it say about woman in her relationship to man?

_____

19. Now what does it say in Proverbs 12:4 about a virtuous woman's relationship to her husband?

_____

20. What do you do with a crown? Where do you wear it?

_____

21. When you put it on your head, do you wrap it up in a burka?

_____

Young women should therefore learn to adorn themselves, to be *beautiful*, *poised*, and *graceful*. Putting all this together, we should see what mature femininity looks like. Girls should have a sense of true authority in the realm that God gave them to rule. They need to learn how to exercise that authority—this means learning how to have a sweet and submissive demeanor, while at the same time being able to boss the boys. Second, it is clear that God thinks that it is "not good" for man to have to fend for himself. Women were created to help men; this is because men need help. At the same time, woman fills man. Third, part of the reason man needs help is that God told him to multiply and fill the earth, which he cannot do by himself. He needs the help of a life-giver. Fourth, wise women have a long and honored history in Scripture, so much so that the personification of wisdom in Proverbs is feminine. And last, women are described as man's glory. Do men have a glory? Yes, and women are it.

RELATIONSHIPS

A good way to summarize the formation of a relationship would be this: if you know what you're doing, do it. If you don't know what you're doing, don't do it.

Biblical courtship is not "a technique." It is not a step-by-step process for garnering sure-fire results every time. Rather, biblical courtship is an area of our lives where, once again, we are called to walk in wisdom.

1. Look up Colossians 3:18–21. First, what are wives told to do?

_____

2. What are husbands told to do?

_____

3. What are they told to *not* do?

_____

4. Dependent children are told to do what?

_____

5. In what areas?

_____

6. What does the Lord think of this?

_____

Now this text is general. That is, it does not give us the "subject matter" under discussion in any given instance. There in Colossae, the husbands and wives, children and fathers, could have been talking about *anything*. So this means that we may apply what is said here to the subject of courtship. And this is an area where strong feelings run deep, and they often run contrary to each other. Those feelings include love, aversion, suspicion, bitterness, and so on.

We also have to guard against waiting for the other guy to go first. When we read a passage like this, the husbands tend to hear the word "submit," wives hear the word "love," parents hear the word "obey," and the children hear "provoke not." It ought not to go this way. Rather, the wives should hear the word "submit," the husbands "love," the children "obey," and fathers "provoke not." This should remind us of Ambrose Bierce's definition of a Christian—someone who believes the New Testament is a divinely inspired book, admirably suited to the spiritual needs of his neighbor. One who follows the teachings of Christ so long as it is consistent with a life of sin.

Courtship requires great wisdom on the part of everybody. But whenever we call for someone else to be obedient *first*, we are abandoning the path of wisdom. Consider yourself, lest you also be tempted. Get the beam out of your own eye first—mothers, fathers, sons, and daughters.

So let's first address the question of principles and methods. Many in the Christian world have adopted what is now called the courtship model. This is just fine, and as a model, as something on paper, it is clearly superior to the common system of recreational dating. But also, on paper, it doesn't do anything. Truth on paper is not really truth at all. Truth must be embodied, just as the Lord Jesus took on flesh, in order to even be itself.

"Method thinking" looks like this: "The first thing a man needs to do is talk to the dad, right? After that, what does he do? Talk to his wife? His daughter? How long before he gets back to the young man? When we have him over to dinner, where does he sit?" It thinks of life as a paint-by-numbers kit.

We also have to remember what we learned about the genesis of quarrels. When considering how we come to quarrel with one another, James tells us that it is because of how we *want*. Driven by want, we come readily, naturally into conflict. And when there is conflict, a reasonable question to ask is "What want brought this about?"

7. Look up James 4:1–3. What causes conflict?

_____

8. And do people ever have such strong desires when it comes to members of the opposite sex? This is not a trick question.

_____

The "wanting" that is related to sex and romance is one of the most powerful wants we have. This means that unless this is surrendered to God, according to His Word, we are setting ourselves up for some fierce quarrels. But note: The wanting is not just on the part of the young couple, wanting to be with each other. The parents have their own desires which can be tangled up with other issues like money or reputation. And parents need to remember that by their actions they are always granting some kind of covenantal permission.

This is not an area where the Golden Rule somehow does not apply. The basis of a godly relationship is a character, in two people, that puts the interests of the other first. The man sacrifices himself for her; she sacrifices herself for him. He gives her what God says she needs. She renders to him what God commands. God is the source of all wisdom, so we can trust Him in this.

With regard to character, marriage does not change what you are; it amplifies what you are. Courtship does not solve all your problems; rather, it gives your character a new opportunity to display itself in a new setting. Are you ready to respect a husband? Then show it through how you respect your father. Are you ready to love a wife? Then show it through how you love your mother. And always remember that obedience is *not* to start in the next chapter of your life. This means that young men and young women should be engaged in the pursuit of becoming the kind of person that the kind of person they would want to marry would want to marry.

DIFFERENCES BETWEEN GUYS AND GIRLS

So we have considered the different aspects of men and women according to the Scriptures. Now obviously this will have an impact on how we understand how they are to relate to one another. And if men and women should relate to one another in a particular way, then this means that the young men and young women should be *learning* how to do this.

It is important to learn this the right way, because going the wrong way can be a lot of fun—for a very short time. Falling off a cliff can feel like flying—or a very short time. The relationship that God created to exist between a man and woman is the best kind of earthly relationship there is, and the counterfeits of this can approximate that "best" feeling, but the end is usually disastrous.

1. Look up Ephesians 5:25–28. What are husbands told to do for their wives?

_____

2. This love is compared to what other kind of love?

_____

3. What does Jesus do for the Church in v. 26?

_____

4. What is the end result? What does the bride of Christ look like as a result of being loved in this way?

_____

5. If a man loves his wife this way, then who does he also love?

_____

6. Look up Proverbs 14:12 and 16:25. There is a way that seems *what* unto a man?

_____

7. But the end is what?

_____

8. Now look up Proverbs 5:3–5. Is the woman in v. 3 attractive?

_____

9. So what is the nature of the caution?

_____

10. What should you consider?

_____

And so this is all said as an encouragement to prepare for this slowly and deliberately. One of the best ways to do this is by learning how guys and girls think, first from Scripture, then from your parents and family, and last in your own experience in groups. When you are in groups, you are not paired off, and yet you can learn an awful lot about how the opposite sex thinks and behaves. This is a whole lot easier if you realize that God made them this way, and they are not doing what they are doing in order to irritate you.

11. In the space below, draw two vertical lines, side by side, with about three inches between them. This is what we might call the "zone of vulnerability." All guys are on one side, and all girls are on the other. If a guy and a girl get into the zone, this means that if they "break up," somebody gets hurt. That is what vulnerability means—woundability. God wants us to live there, but because it is risky, He wants us to be protected by means of a covenant—which is what marriage is.

12. Look up 1 Timothy 5:1–2. What does Paul tell Timothy to be very careful to do?

_____

13. Look up 1 Corinthians 11:9. Who was created for whom?

_____

14. Now look a few verses down. In vv. 11–12, does this mean that men can be independent of women?

_____

Guys are task oriented, and girls are guy oriented. God created man to tend and work the garden, and He created the woman to tend and work the man. So this means that a woman should be helping a man with his goals, not trying to distract him away from them. And this means that a man should welcome the help of a woman, and not regard it as a nuisance. And of course, for those of you who are not married, you can practice on your dad and brothers, or your mom and sisters. And of course, to a lesser degree, you can also practice on your classmates.

Because God created men "for the task," and woman "for the man," this means that men tend to be more analytic, and women tend to be lateral and relational. This is not so that we might have something to criticize in the other, but rather so that we can see where to invest our gifts.

Remember that men are built to be deliverers, and women are built to be nurturers. This means that men are life savers while women are life givers. This is all a design feature. The differences are not there because something has gone terribly, horribly wrong. Like two completely different notes that harmonize with one another, so guys and girls are completely different notes—but if they hit their pitch, the results are great.

DEFINING COOL

There are some issues that are important for us to address, but we would have trouble using a Bible concordance looking that issue up. A good example is the idea of the cool, and then a particular practice that we may treat as something of a lab—that practice being the biblical attitude toward tattoos. Every generation has to deal with new manifestations of cool—actually, it is getting to the point where we have to deal with new manifestations of it every fifteen minutes—so the issue of tattoos is just one block of wood we have picked up, but the real point is to learn how to whittle.

We have to set certain things aside right at the first. We are talking about coolness as an important *cultural* category, and not addressing it as a term of generic approval. "These snow tires at Les Schwab were a really good deal." "Cool." The cultural category I have in mind is that which uses it as a term of approval or acceptance at the most fundamental level available. Consequently, I want to define the idea of *cool* as a type of secular justification. As is inescapable with all forms of attempted counterfeit justification, an attempt to have it be *by faith alone* is also necessary. What elements that surround justification are present?

- Antithesis—there is always another side to the divide, the uncool, the damned.

- The formalists—a bunch of people who are *not* cool want to be cool anyhow, and so they keep joining the church. The cool, like the early Christians, are victims of their own success.

- *Semper reformanda*—there has to be a constant winnowing. The god of Cool raises up a new vanguard, and *they* are the cutting, bleeding edge. And then about fifteen days later, every pimply junior high kid in America has one. Shoot.

- Assumes the center—the definers of cool assume that they are in charge of the universe.

- Vindicated—the Christian who is justified is declared righteous, despite his sins, which are many and grievous. Righteousness is imputed. The same privilege, the same *status*, is given to the cool by the arbiters and worshippers of cool. Who even cares if the iconic James Dean had personal problems, or if Marilyn Monroe was a bundle of neuroses?

- Attitude—many might say, "I can't define it, but I know it when I see it." Some sunglasses are cool, some just keep the sun out. Some hair gels are cool, some are just goopy. What is it that makes it cool or not? Attitude; faith. Show me your faith by your works.

Are sunglasses a thing indifferent? Sure, as Calvin would say (*Institutes* 3.19): "I admit it, provided they are used indifferently." But if there is an attitude, if there is ostentatious display, if there is spin on it, a little English, then the biblical name for this is *worldliness*.

1. Look up 1 John 2:15–17. We are commanded to not love two things. What are they?

_____

2. If a man loves the world, what can we say about him?

_____

3. There are three things that are described as being "in the world." What are they?

_____

4. Look up Genesis 3:6. What three things attracted Eve to the forbidden fruit?

_____

5. Can you see any correlation between the passage in 1 John and this Genesis passage?

_____

6. Back in 1 John 2:17, what passes away, and what abides forever?

_____

This does not at all mean that we cannot enjoy the things in the world. The issue is the things *of* the world. Calvin again: "And we have never been forbidden to laugh, or to be filled, or to join new possessions to old or ancestral ones, or to delight in musical harmony, or to drink wine . . . away with vanity and arrogance—in order that men may with a clean conscience cleanly use God's gifts" (*Institutes* 3.19). So excluding actions explicitly prohibited by God, worldliness is defined by attitude, and not by whether the item is on an *index prohibitum*. All things are lawful, but not all things are necessary.

Someone secure in their Christian identity, when enticed by the latest worldly thing, will ask, "Why?" This is in sharp contrast to the question asked by unthinking teenagers everywhere, which is, "Why not?"

The next thing to remember is that there is no place in the world where we can go in order to opt out of that basic choice. Whatever we do, whether we eat or drink, we are to do it to the glory of God (1 Cor. 10:31). And remember, in sorting this out we are not permitted to read the Bible *only*. We must also read the culture accurately. We have to read the menu at God's restaurant, and we also have to read the menu at the *devil's* restaurant, in order to know what we are *not* going to order.

- An Israelite dancing around the golden calf who saw Moses and armed Levites approaching would not have the option of saying, "But I wasn't *worshiping* . . . I just like to dance! Kickin' band they got here . . . um."
- A modern Christian doesn't have the right to talk to his pious grandmother with an obscenity-laced tirade, on the grounds that the apostle Paul didn't know *any* of those words, and hence could not have had them in mind in Ephesians 5:4.

All this said, let's consider a particular case study.

7. Look up Leviticus 19:28. Two things are prohibited. What are they?

Let's begin with some incidental remarks about tattoos, before moving on to an application of this idea of the justified *cool*. Some people say the verse from Leviticus doesn't apply because it says "for the *dead*." But how many modern tattoos *are* for the dead? Why do we refuse to see deep patterns here? Tattooed tears for men killed? In memory of? Obviously, this verse ought not to be applied like a verse that fell from the sky—otherwise, someone could well ask why I don't have Hasidic ringlets, and why my beard is trimmed (Lev. 19:27). We are looking at a narrative, and in the story of lost humanity, *men are always seeking justification*. If culture is religion externalized, it is reasonable to ask what religion this is. Another category is what we might describe as simply unfortunate—the sorority girl who gets a tramp stamp on her lower back. It is an ancient Chinese character which, when translated, means "stupid white girl."

In the old covenant, only one cutting was permitted, and that was the required cutting of circumcision (Gen. 17:10). In the new covenant, with the replacement of circumcision with baptism (Col. 2:11), that number is lowered to zero. You have a mark on your body already—you have been baptized. Piercings are a sign of subordination (as with a godly wife in Ezek. 16:12), or with slavery (Deut. 15:16–17). Make up and other decorative adornings are temporary and are certainly lawful as long as they are not overdone (1 Tim. 2:9). Markings on houses, cars, and tee-shirts are also lawful (Deut. 11:18). But your body was purchased, which means you are not to rent out, lease, or sell advertising space on it.

To mark your body with any other "ultimate commitment" marks is to reveal that in your mind and heart you believe that your baptism needs supplements. In other words, you are either getting a worldly tattoo, or you are getting an "I love Jesus" tattoo. If the former, we are told not to seek justification in the world by the world. This is part of the world's system of marking her sons, and we are not to be worldly. But if you want to show your radical dedication to Christ, what exactly did you think was deficient with your baptism?

AUTHENTICITY

When we talk about the way we dress, we often forget that we are speaking about language. That is, we use the full force of language to get what we want to get, and when called on it, we then "plead the dictionary." Suppose a young rebel in your church were out in the parking lot after services, loudly yelling what we euphemistically call the f-word. When someone, Mrs. Grundy say, remonstrates with him, he retreats to the study of etymology and linguistics, saying that the original Anglo-Saxon was entirely innocent, and that in Chinese these particular sounds mean something like *doorknob*. Shouldn't nobody have a problem, sez he. Yes, says Mrs. Grundy, legalism banging away on all eight cylinders, but that is not what this word means *here*.

Every culture has "good clothes," clothes you wear to a wedding or a funeral, or when the queen asks you to sing for her. Whatever those are (and we shouldn't care what those are), wear that kind of thing to church. That is appropriate. Every culture has the equivalent of coveralls for changing the oil in the car, or carrying honey buckets. So don't wear those. Just like different cultures have different languages and combinations of letters and sounds, so they have different ways of communicating respect and honor. Those who wear the clothing of rebellion, precisely because it is rebellious, and then try to pretend (in certain settings) that this is just stitched fabric, nothing more and nothing less, are showing how deeply the lies of lowlife authenticity have affected us. It is manifestly not true, and everyone conspires to act as though it is true.

This is why affected authenticity should drive us up the wall. You want to see a Pharisee with widened phylacteries? Look for someone who bought jeans with the holes already in them. And then ask yourself the question, "What would Jesus do?" From all available evidence, He would laugh and make fun of it. So when Christians gather for worship, which indicates their *submission* to God, they ought not to be wearing clothes that proclaim (as everyone knows they proclaim) *rebellion*. Sure, the Bible never says that we can't wear goth and paint our fingernails black. It also never says that you can't give Mrs. Grundy the bird, as you lay rubber out of the parking lot.

1. Look up Matthew 23:5. When Jesus chastises the Pharisees here, what was their basic problem?

2. What did they do in order to be noticed by men?

_____

Note: a phylactery was something that Pharisees would tie onto their foreheads or hands, containing sentences from the law.

3. Now are there different ways that this same problem could be exhibited, without using phylacteries or borders of garments at all? For example, like "my Bible is more underlined than yours"? Give your own example.

_____

In any society, certain things are valued. In those societies, there is an immediate pressure to have "the look" of that thing, without actually having it. In the Middle East, men can buy make up to rub on their forehead so that it will *look* like they have been praying toward Mecca the required five times a day. But in the secular West, the ideal is different, so we fake something else. Is it possible to buy pre-ripped jeans (with an extra charge), but which also have paint spatters all over them? Why, yes, it is. Now *who buys this stuff?* We should narrow it down to hypocrites or buffoons, that's who, and perhaps both.

Suppose we marketed a line of aprons that already had the pancake batter encrusted on them, or perhaps spaghetti pre-stains. People who buy this kind of stuff are buying a prefab authenticity, plastic authenticity, lying authenticity, cool authenticity, too-much-discretionary-income authenticity, and are as hollow as a jug. But one other thing—the prefab factory-fresh grime is really obvious when you look straight at it. But it is not any *more* authentic to rip your own jeans, splatter your own paint, in order to go slouch around at your grandmother's funeral. Then we are just talking about the difference between mass-marketed lies and homemade ones.

The problem of Pharisaism is not solved by dropping the phylactery that is "wider than yours" and picking up the Bible that is "more underlined than yours." You cannot solve spiritual problems of the heart simply by rearranging the furniture. We are born casting sidelong glances, and the solution to this is *repentance*, not really cool sunglasses that hide what our eyes are doing, or an iPod to keep us from hearing what the prophets are saying. These are difficult days to be a satirist, and so I hesitate with the reductios for fear that somebody would think the following is a good idea. But here goes anyway. What would we think if someone started manufacturing pre-underlined Bibles, or prayer jeans with just the knees ripped out? We could sell them as "prayer warrior" jeans. This is the essence of Pharisaism, and it is not difficult to identify.

Every culture esteems certain things, and then we always have to deal with the posers and hosers who try to get the glory for having those things when they do not even come close.

This is true in all places and all times, and applies to everything that can be esteemed. Sweater vests, suit coats, flowing robes, whatever. When Jesus attacked the Pharisees, He was attacking them for being *phony*. And our culture is filled with phonies, posing as authentic rebel souls. We should not accuse them of being *doctrinal* Pharisees—but rather of being phonies, just like the Pharisees. And the Pharisees could not defend themselves by demanding to see a verse from the Torah that condemns phylacteries wider than seven centimeters, or a verse that specifically condemns flowing robes, or blowing trumpets on street corners. Nor could they ward off the critique by demanding "just how long does a prayer in the synagogue have to be to qualify as a sin under 'lengthy.'"

Now the point of my critique is not that such dumb stuff is limited to modern pop culture. This is a standing human problem. But in certain times and eras, the problem is accentuated, as it is in ours. This is because first-century Pharisaism was self-consciously elitist, and the whole idea was to be a disciplined corps. If you limit the number of people in the club, you (by definition) limit the number of possible hypocrites in the club. But in our era we are dealing with mass-marketed authenticity, off-the-rack authenticity, everyman-regardless authenticity, lonely-soul authenticity, blow-dried authenticity, three-dollar-bill authenticity, and, as they say on television, much, much, more.

Let me point out the obvious once more. Imagine trying to explain pre-degraded, ripped, and splattered clothing to Virgil, Jonathan Edwards, Boethius, George Washington, or the venerable Bede. You are not having to explain this to a greatly amused critic, like me, but to someone who has never heard of such a thing, and is honestly and naively curious. Your assignment, should you choose to accept it, is to explain to them why you buy clothing that pre-distressed for you, and you are willing to pay *more* for the privilege. We have *factories* that will wreck your clothes for you, and lots of people say, "*Oooo*, gotta have it." So they can get to retail outlets, this kind of clothing is driven around the United States in *trucks*. We should be open to other possibilities (honestly), but thus far the only answers seem to be that such a customer is either a hypocrite or a dope.

And let us acknowledge (again) that every culture and subculture has its hypocrites and dopes. But the modern subculture of mass-marketed-lonely-poet authenticity has elevated the thing to an art form. And nobody notices! Nobody sees!

The problem with the traditional Christian critique of this stuff is that it plays to the pride. "You're a rebellious slob." And the slob carelessly (and *very* carefully) brushes his hair out of his eyes and says (or thinks), "Yeah, well, Lord Byron was misunderstood too." The traditional critique plays along with the central delusion here. We need to stop accusing these people of marching to a different drummer when, to all appearances, they are as regimented as a drum-and-bugle corps. The problem is not that these people are rebellious slobs, but rather that this is a culture-wide subculture of conformist inauthenticity. It is hypocrisy on stilts.

HANDLING MONEY

For many Christians, the practical issues surrounding money are a real headache. There are questions about acquiring it, about managing it, and about giving it away. But we are not left without instruction—we are to tithe, give, manage, provide, and enjoy.

1. So first look up Matthew 6:19–24. What are we not supposed to do in the first instance?

_____

2. Why not?

_____

3. What are we to do rather instead?

_____

4. And what reason is given?

_____

5. What follows your treasure?

_____

6. What causes your whole body to be full of light or vice versa?

_____

7. What does Jesus say is impossible?

_____

8. And what was God's competitor in this instance?

_____

Jesus teaches us that His followers must not be graspers. They are not to be all about acquisition. Do not lay up earthly treasures (v. 19). You are putting your treasure in an insecure place. Rather, lay up treasure in heaven—the most secure investment possible (v. 20). Jesus tells us that our heart will be wherever our treasure is (v. 21). From this we can tell where our treasure is—where the heart is. The next expression "if your eye is single" is a Hebrew idiom for "if you are generous." If you are generous, your whole life is blessed (v. 22). Having an evil eye meant that you were miserly. If you are a miser and a tightwad—how great is the darkness (v. 23). The issue is mastery, *possession*. God must be your master, and your money must be a fellow servant, along with you.

So let us begin with the tithe, God's tax. The tithe is not extortion money paid to God, so that you get to keep 90 percent. Rather, it is tribute money, demonstrating that you understand that He really is the possessor of all of it. The tithe is rendered as your way of saying that you understand yourself to be simply a steward of the remainder.

Some wonder about the tithe in the times of the new covenant. First, we believe that the Old Testament is binding unless the New Testament says that it isn't—as we see, for example, with animal sacrifices. But if a biblical principle is not fulfilled in the New, then our operating assumption is that it continues. But for those who find this insufficient, demanding that a practice must be explicitly taught in the New for Christians to be bound to it, let us consider 1 Corinthians 9:13–14.

9. Look that passage up. How were those who preached the gospel to live?

_____

The Old Testament priests lived off the tithe, and St. Paul requires that those who preach the gospel should live *in the same way.*

The second measure is this. The Bible links the first table of the law to the second.

10. Look up 1 John 4:20. If we don't love our neighbor, what can we not say?

_____

In the earlier text, Jesus mentions the need for personal generosity. That would include donations of time, work, money, gifts, advice. All of these are ways of *giving yourself away.* As God has given to us (freely), and we have returned it to Him (*freely*), let us also be generous to those assigned by God to us in that noble office of "neighbor." Is the first instinct to hoard? Is the first instinct to say no? Is the first instinct to pull away?

BASIC CHRISTIAN LIVING

11. Look up Proverbs 11:25. What happens to a generous person?

_____

12. What happens to him in Proverbs 22:9?

_____

13. And what is the final lot of the generous person in Isaiah 32:7–8?

_____

The third measure is shrewdness. The second and third must go together, and they must go together in this order—generous and then shrewd. Not shrewd and then stingy. The right kind of shrewdness is demonstrated in an understanding of the source of God's blessing, and wisdom in the management of it. You give to get, in order to be able to give again. A foolish man can be "generous" if he drives down the road, throwing money out the window. But that is not true generosity.

14. What are we told to do in Proverbs 27:23?

_____

Put this another way—know the value and importance of what you are giving away, and _give it away anyway_. As John Wesley put it once, "Earn all you can, save all you can, give all you can."

The fourth measure is provision for your people. We want to provide for our own, and then be generous with whatever is left over. This is backwards. You are to be generous _in such a way_ that you are more than able to provide for those that God has given you responsibility for.

15. Yes, you must provide, and please look up 1 Timothy 5:8. What is the condition of someone who doesn't provide?

_____

But what do I mean—_in such a way_? Seek first the kingdom and all these things will be added to you (Mt. 6:33). And you should prayerfuly consider that this encompasses more than just next month's rent.

16. What does a good man do for his grandchildren (Prov. 13:22)?

_____

And the last measure is this: *enjoy* yourself.

17. Look up 1 Timothy 6:17. Why does God give us wealth?

_____

The idolater has enough food but no taste buds. The grateful Christian can taste God's goodness.

18. Look up Deut. 8:17. Why does God give us the power to get wealth?

_____

19. And why should we rejoice before God (Deut. 12:7)?

_____

20. When God judged the Israelites, what was the judgment for (Deut. 28:47–48)?

_____

DEALING WITH FEAR

We are talking about "dealing with fear," but we could title this a bunch of other things as well. It could be called "inescapable fear," or "freedom from fear," or "the Christian grace of fear." But this requires some unpacking.

1. To begin our study of fear, look up Luke 12:4–7. Jesus commands us not to fear a particular group. Who are they?

_____

2. Why should we not fear them?

_____

3. Whom should we fear?

_____

4. Why?

_____

5. What additional reason is given for not being fearful?

_____

Notice how Jesus addresses His disciples here—He calls them His *friends* (v. 4). His next words are instructions to them to not be afraid of those whose maximum power is that of physical death (v. 4). He then turns to the subject of the one that they should fear—the one who has complete and full authority over hell. Christ emphasizes that they should fear Him— He says it three times in one verse. *Fear Him* (v. 5). God remembers even the sparrows, sold so cheaply in the market (v. 6). This means that the hairs of your head are all numbered (v. 7). Do not fear, therefore, because you are worth more than many sparrows (v. 7).

Here is the pattern—fear not, fear, fear not. We are not to fear men. All *they* can do is kill us. We are to fear God—He is the one who can throw people into hell. But God loves us and cherishes us and cares deeply for us. We should therefore not fear the providences of God concerning us. Still less should we fear the pains of hell.

6. Look up 1 John 4:18. What does love do to fear?

_____

7. Why?

_____

We do not fear hell; we defy it. We do not fear hell, because we fear the one who can put us there. Because we fear Him, we know that He does not want to do this to us—we are worth more than many sparrows. When He sends His angels they almost always say, "Fear *not*."

Now this is why we have spoken about inescapable fear. If we fear man, we do not fear God. If we fear God, we will not fear man. But we *will* fear someone. The question, therefore, is not *whether* we will fear, but rather *whom* we will fear. This is just another form of "not whether, but which."

Scripture describes a healthy kind of fear. One of the central reasons why modern Christians are so timid is because we have not cultivated a healthy fear of God.

8. For example, what is the beginning of knowledge (Prov. 1:7)?

_____

This is foundational. And notice how fear of God is described in the New Testament as a glorious and wonderful thing.

9. How did the witnesses of the empty tomb depart from there (Mt. 28:8)?

_____

10. What rests upon those who fear the Lord (Lk. 1:50)?

_____

11. What three things went together when the people saw Jesus heal the paralytic (Lk. 5:26; cf. 7:16)?

_____

12. What two things did the early church combine in their walk (Acts 9:31)?

_____

_____

13. What does the fear of God enable us to perfect (2 Cor. 7:1)?

_____

_____

14. How are we to work out our salvation (Phil. 2:12–13)?

_____

_____

15. How can we submit to one another (Eph. 5:21)?

_____

_____

16. What should our worship of God be like (Heb. 12:28–29)?

_____

_____

There are many other passages like this—this is a point that could be multiplied many times over. The fear of God is a good thing, and is accompanied by many good things. In our fear of God, we begin to *know*; fear and *great joy* mingle in knowledge of the resurrection; fear receives *mercy*; fear renders *awe and glory*; walking in fear means *walking in comfort*; fear advances *personal holiness*; fear works out *salvation*; fear enables us in cultivating the spirit of *mutual submission* and *humility*; fear animates *appropriate worship*. Fear of God is a Christian's glory.

This kind of fear banishes another kind of fear. Because of this profound and all-pervasive fear, we do not need to fear *anything*. "For God hath not given us *the spirit of fear*, but of power, and of love, and of a sound mind" (2 Tim. 1:7). "For ye have not received *the spirit of bondage again to fear*, but ye have received the Spirit of adoption" (Rom. 8:15). "And deliver them who *through fear of death* were all their lifetime subject to bondage" (Heb. 2:15).

This means that if you are troubled with anxieties and fears, then you need to name the problem accurately. The problem is that you do *not* fear as you ought, and the vacuum has been filled by many phantoms. Now we are not talking about normal physiological reactions—shaking when you just escaped from a car wreck, or you have a close call with a grizzly bear. We are addressing the ongoing fears that cripple your Christian life and your relationships with others. What does this mean? It refers to fear of slippery roads, loss of reputation, the cancer you might get twenty years out, dying young, marital unhappiness in the future, or any other kind of "what about?" or "what if?" followed by some unpleasantness that you cooked up. The fear of God *liberates*. The fear of the creature *paralyzes*—because to guard effectively against whatever it is, you have to be omnipotent. And you are *not*.

This means that the fear of God is the foundation of all true contentment. *All things* work together for good to those who love God and are the called according to His purpose (Rom. 8:28). And when we are content, free from grasping and covetousness, what may we then say? God will never ditch us. We are His people.

"Let your conversation be without covetousness; and be content with such things as ye have: for he hath said, I will never leave thee, nor forsake thee. So that we may boldly say, The Lord is my helper, *and I will not fear* what man shall do unto me" (Heb. 13:5–6).

SWEET SLEEP

Sleep is an important part of our lives, even though we can recall very little of it. We spend about a third of our lives asleep, which amounts to twenty-five years for a seventy-five-year-old man. And if the chief end of our lives is to glorify God and enjoy Him forever, as the Shorter Catechism puts it, this necessarily includes our sleep. And when we turn to the Bible for instruction, we are not disappointed.

1. Look up Proverbs 3:21–24. What should not depart from a young man's eyes?

_____

2. What will be life to his soul, and grace to his neck?

_____

3. What will happen as he walks along the way?

_____

4. What will not happen as he lies down?

_____

5. What will happen?

_____

The author of Proverbs is instructing his son on the value of wisdom and discretion. Keep them in full view at all times (v. 21). They are the life of your soul; treat them that way (v. 22). They are grace hanging around your neck (v. 22). When you do this, you will walk prudently and be safe; you will not stumble (v. 23). The crown of this series of blessings is this—when you lie down, you will not be afraid of what might happen while you are in that defenseless state. When you lie down, *your sleep will be sweet* (v. 24).

We need to begin by fixing a central principle in our minds. Even as Christians, we are broken sinners in various stage of repair. God is fitting us for heaven, and He is doing it His way. Some require drastic treatment, while others do not appear to need that. God's blessings and chastisements—within the covenant—are His instruments for doing so. Now as children of the covenant, we are authorized to pursue the blessings He offers, and we must pursue them. But we have no right to *demand* them in accordance with our own schedules or timetables. Part of what we learn is that when we seek a blessing from God, we are necessarily seeking everything that goes with that blessing.

6. Look up Psalm 127:1–2. What can a man not do by himself?

_____

7. If God acts on his behalf, what will he receive?

_____

This is one of the great blessings of the covenant. Pursue it fully, and all its scriptural commandments, but do not demand it in your own name.

8. What happens if God lifts up the light of His countenance upon us (Ps. 4:6–8)?

_____

We must begin by assuming certain things as given. The first is that God does *not* sleep. Because God does not sleep, you may. "Behold, he that keepeth Israel shall neither slumber nor sleep. The LORD is thy keeper: the LORD is thy shade upon thy right hand" (Ps. 121:4–5).

Another way of putting this is that a restful sleep is one of the best possible metaphors for faith, trust. The "letting go" that is involved in sleep is just the way we ought to be with God all the time. And when you are wound way too tight, the result is a sleep that is not very much like a sleep—tossing and turning all night. Sleep is to be like trust; sleep is to *be* trust.

One of the most striking things about Scripture's teaching on sleep is the fact that sleep and death are so often compared. And keep the previous point about sleep and faith in mind. Sleep, death, and faith all should involve a basic *surrender to God*. "And the LORD said unto Moses, Behold, thou shalt sleep with thy fathers" (Deut. 31:16; cf. 2 Sam. 7:12). "For now shall I sleep in the dust; and thou shalt seek me in the morning, but I shall not be" (Job 7:21). "And many of them that sleep in the dust of the earth shall awake, some to everlasting life, and some to shame and everlasting contempt" (Dan. 12:2). "Howbeit Jesus spake of his death: but they thought that he had spoken of taking of rest in sleep" (Jn. 11:13). "For David, after he had served his own generation by the will of God, fell on sleep, and was laid unto his fathers, and saw corruption" (Acts 13:36). This is far more than a convenient metaphor. There is a deep reality here.

But sometimes sleep is not a good thing. The Bible teaches that there are people under a judicial stupor, a judgment sleep sent from God. "For the LORD hath poured out upon you the spirit of deep sleep, and hath closed your eyes: the prophets and your rulers, the seers hath he covered" (Is. 29:10). "Therefore let us not sleep, as do others; but let us watch and be sober. For they that sleep sleep in the night; and they that be drunken are drunken in the night. But let us, who are of the day, be sober, putting on the breastplate of faith and love; and for an helmet, the hope of salvation. For God hath not appointed us to wrath, but to obtain salvation by our Lord Jesus Christ, Who died for us, that, whether we wake or sleep, we should live together with him" (1 Thess. 5:6–10; cf. Rom. 13:11–14).

Sleep is always either obedient or disobedient. How can that be?, you might ask. Well, you either should be or you shouldn't be. Obedience to God encompasses every aspect of our lives, including how and when we sleep. "Love not sleep, lest thou come to poverty; open thine eyes, and thou shalt be satisfied with bread" (Prov. 20:13). "And said unto them, Why sleep ye? rise and pray, lest ye enter into temptation" (Lk. 22:46). "Slothfulness casteth into a deep sleep; and an idle soul shall suffer hunger" (Prov. 19:15; cf. 6:9–11; 24:33–34).

Here are some practical suggestions. First, learn to see sleeping as obedient discipleship. It is not the time for you to "check out," in order to clock back in as a disciple in the morning. Second, look forward to each morning as a small resurrection, a type of the resurrection. That is what it is. Third, look for God's blessing in that resurrection (Gen. 2:21–22). Fourth, seek first the kingdom of God in the day before you seek to sleep. "I will not give sleep to mine eyes, or slumber to mine eyelids, Until I find out a place for the LORD" (Ps. 132:4–5). And fifth, work like you really believed there was such a thing as the Puritan work ethic. "The sleep of a labouring man is sweet, whether he eat little or much: but the abundance of the rich will not suffer him to sleep" (Eccl. 5:12).

IN SUMMARY

As we think about what we have covered in this course, let's review just a few things from most of the chapters.

1. First, we want to make sure that our Christian life is God-centered. His glory is more important than our happiness, and the only basis for our true happiness is to know and acknowledge this. Look up Isaiah 6:1–8, and read through it carefully. If worship is presenting yourself to God for service, and not simply being awestruck at His glory, where does the worship in this passage occur? How is the idea of worship communicated?

_____

2. Before God sends Isaiah out, He sends angels to cleanse his lips. This is important. Look up Hebrews 10:16–18. There are two main characteristics of the new covenant that are mentioned. What are they?

_____

3. What two things happen if we confess our sins to God (1 Jn. 1:8–10)?

_____

4. Now look up Leviticus 6:1–7, and read it through carefully. Now in the fourth verse, what is the basic duty that a man has if he has done this sort of thing?

_____

5. According to 1 John 5:13, why did John write to those who believe?

_____

6. If he wants them to know this, is it reasonable to assume that it is possible to know?

_____

7. According to 1 Corinthians 10:13, will God ever allow us to be locked up in temptation, with no way out except by sinning?

_____

8. Look up Deuteronomy 8:3. Why should we be committed to intelligent Bible reading? What is the basis of man's life? What is not?

_____

9. What should be the point of our conversation (Eph. 4:29)?

_____

10. Now let's look up Philippians 4:6–7. According to this passage, what should make us anxious?

_____

11. When we work, who should we remember is watching (Col. 2:23)?

_____

12. Look up James 4:1-3. What does James want us to understand the origins of?

_____

13. What does the Bible say about the spirit that dwells in us?

_____

14. Look up Luke 14:7-11. From that passage, explain why Jesus told this parable. What did He notice?

_____

15. According to His teaching, what should we not do at a wedding?

_____

16. So what approach should we take to the seats of honor?

_____

17. Is the lesson here to never sit in a seat of honor? If not, what is the lesson?

_____

18. Look up 1 John 2:15–17. We are commanded to not love two things. What are they?

_____

19. There are three things that are described as being "in the world." What are they?

_____

20. Look up Genesis 3:6. What three things attracted Eve to the forbidden fruit?

_____

21. Look up Proverbs 11:25. What happens to a generous person?

_____

22. Now turn to Luke 12:4–7. Jesus commands us not to fear a particular group. Who are they?

_____

23. Why should we not fear them?

_____

24. Whom should we fear?

_____

25. Look up Proverbs 3:21–24. What should not depart from a young man's eyes?

_____

26. What will not happen as he lies down?

_____

27. What will happen?

_____

28. In all these things, whom should we always trust?

_____

Basic Answers to the Study Questions

Note to the reader: These answers are not intended to answer the questions throughout this book exhaustively. Instead, use these answers as a guide or a starting place for composing or checking your own answers. By all means feel free to bring in other portions of Scripture or other thoughts as appropriate.

Answers for Lesson 1: The Nature of Worship

1. Look up Isaiah 6:1–8, and read through it carefully. If worship is presenting yourself to God for service, and not simply being awestruck at His glory, where does the worship in this passage occur? How is the idea of worship communicated?

The worship occurs in verse 8. Instead of simply remaining in the awe of verse 5, Isaiah answers God's question by offering to serve God himself as his messenger.

2. Now look up Deuteronomy 6:13 and compare it to Matthew 4:10. The command is to worship the Lord your God and serve Him only. Satan wanted Christ's worship (i.e., service). In these passages, when we make ourselves available to God for His service, what instruments of mine am I presenting to Him?

We're offering every area of our lives: lying, walking, speaking; it's all God's (even down to what's written on the walls). Satan didn't mind if Jesus was a king, just so long as Jesus's "being" was subordinate to Satan.

3. Now in Romans 12:1–2, worship is the offering up of the physical body as a living sacrifice. What will the consequence of such worship be on the attitudes of the ones offering it (v. 3)?

Instead of being arrogant and inflated, our opinions of ourselves will be sober-minded.

4. Romans 6:19 presents another angle on worship. What is offered there, and as what?

Our body parts will be offered as "slaves of righteousness."

5. Having done all this, praise is certainly appropriate. According to Psalm 33:1, for whom is praise appropriate?

Praise is fitting for the upright.

6. Under girded by faithful worship, when is praise appropriate? According to Psalm 34:1 and Hebrews 13:15, when should we praise the Lord?

David says praise is fitting at all times (even when he was pretending to be crazy in the Philistine court). Hebrews says the same: we should continually offer praise to God.

7. What should we conclude about when we should be worshiping the Lord?

We should be offering ourselves constantly to the Lord.

8. God reigns, and what is called to rejoice (97:1)?

The earth and all the islands are told to rejoice.

9. His holiness is not what we might assume—His righteousness and judgment are compared to what (v. 2)?

They're compared to clouds and darkness surrounding the Lord's throne.

10. A fire precedes Him, and so what happens to His enemies (v. 3)?

They are burned up all around Him.

11. Lightning flashes, and the whole created order sees it, and what is the response (v. 4)?

The proper response is being afraid enough to tremble.

12. In the presence of God, hills and mountains melt in what way (v. 5)?

They melt like pooling wax.

13. The heavens preach, and what does everyone sees as a result (v. 6)?

Everybody sees the glory of God.

14. A curse is pronounced—confounded be all false worshipers. And what are all the gods summoned to do (v. 7)?

They too are called to worship the Lord.

15. When this is proclaimed, Zion hears and is glad. What do the daughters of Judah do (v. 8)?

The daughters of Judah rejoice.

16. Why do we rejoice (v. 9)?

We rejoice because God is much more exalted than all the other gods, and way above the earth.

17. This transcendent sense of true worship has potent ethical ramifications—what are those who love the Lord called to hate (v. 10)?

We must hate evil.

18. In this setting, there are those who return the hatred. What does God do (v. 10)?

He saves His people from the wicked and preserves them.

19. Light is sown for the righteous. Who receives gladness (v. 11)?

The upright in heart receive gladness.

20. We are summoned by God to therefore rejoice. What are we to do as we remember His holiness (v. 12)?

We give thanks as we remember His holiness.

21. Describe in a few words the difference between praise and worship.

[Answers may vary] Praise flows directly out of worship, and can only happen when we have caught a glimpse of Who God is and have offered ourselves to Him for His purposes—because of that, we respond with the fear and trembling and rejoicing and gladness of praise. Worship is presenting yourself for service.

22. Describe the relation between a perception of God's holiness and the right kind of worship.

[Answers may vary] If we misunderstand God's holiness, we will be either falsely strict (moralists) or falsely lax (libertines). A right perception of God's holiness leads to trembling, thankfulness, hatred of evil, rejection of idols, and eventually inheriting of the earth.

Answers for Lesson 2: Forgiveness of Sin

1. Look up Matthew 1:19–21, a passage which records the dream that Joseph received. Why was Jesus named *Jesus*? What was the point?

He was named Jesus *because He was going to save people from sins—the point is that He's going to be saving.*

2. Now look up Hebrews 10:16–18. There are two main characteristics of the new covenant that are mentioned there. What are they?

Instead of external stone commandments, God will put His law in the hearts and minds of the people of the new covenant. Second, He won't remember His people's sins any more.

3. So again, what does the name *Jesus* mean?

Jesus *means "Savior."*

4. What does the new covenant promise us?

The new covenant promises remission of sins and internalization of God's law.

5. So look up Matthew 9:12. Who did Jesus come for?

Jesus came to heal sick people..

6. If Jesus came for messed up people, then can you disqualify yourself from His grace by being all messed up?

Certainly not—you must be messed up in order to be fixed.

7. Think of the person you have the *most* trouble loving. Are you willing to ask God to think of you the way you think of them?

[Answers may vary] Because of hypocrisy and pride, that's a really difficult prayer to pray, but it's one that Jesus says we must pray.

8. Look up Acts 5:31. Besides repentance to Israel, what does Jesus give?

He also gives forgiveness of sins.

9. Look up Acts 13:38. Why is Jesus preached?

He is preached because through Him is forgiveness of sins.

10. Look up Acts 26:18. What is the end result of being transferred from the power of Satan to God?

Those who no longer belong to Satan may receive forgiveness of sins and an inheritance with the rest of the faithful.

11. In Ephesians 1:7 and Colossians 1:14, what is the result of redemption through the blood of Christ?

We have redemption through His grace, which is forgiveness of sins.

12. What sorts of sins might this kind of forgiveness need to cover?

Jesus forgives all sins, and we similarly must forgive others for sins of every kind, large and small.

13. What are they asking you to promise, and what are you promising?

They ask you to promise not to hold the sin against them. Every time you forgive, you promise that you won't.

Answers for Lesson 3: Confession of Sin

1. What do we do if we say we have no sin?
We are deceiving ourselves.

2. What is not in us if we say we have no sin?
The truth is not in us.

3. What two things happen if we confess our sins?
Jesus forgives us our sins, and also cleanses us from all our unrighteousness.

4. What two attributes of God cause this to happen?

God's faithfulness is in the forgiveness, and His justice is involved in the cleansing.

5. What do we say about God if we say we have not sinned?

We say God is a liar.

6. What is not in us?

God's word is not in us.

7. Can the same number of things be spilled or knocked over in two houses, and yet one of the houses is clean and the other filthy?

Yes—the levels of cleanliness depend on if things are cleaned up.

8. In the space below, draw a basic graph, with a vertical axis on the left and a horizontal one along the bottom. Alongside the vertical axis, write the word *joy* and along the horizontal axis write *time*. We are going to graph what a lot of Christian lives look like.

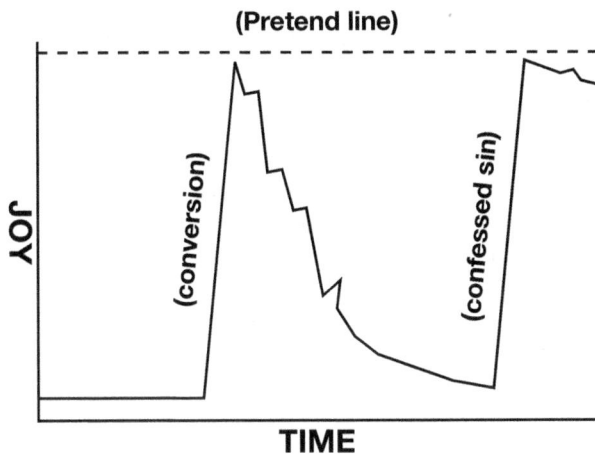

9. You might rationalize. "What I did wasn't really wrong." What does it mean if you are walking around, muttering to yourself that what you did was really, really right?

It means you aren't being honest by calling your action what God calls it: sin. So, you aren't confessing.

10. You might excuse. "What I did was not started by *me*." This is a variation of "what I did was wrong, *but*." What happens to your forgiveness when you say that magic word *but*?

That means you aren't actually "speaking the same" as God, and God won't forgive something you don't confess.

11. You might postpone it. "In *my* honest opinion, the best day for jumping will be sometime tomorrow afternoon." But what happens when you get to tomorrow afternoon? Is confessing then easier or harder?

The same reluctance is there the next day, plus the sins of the extra day, and you still aren't in fellowship with God.

12. You might blame somebody else, anybody else. "I think *they* should be here jumping, not me." When you lie, you think about your lie. When someone lies about you, and you get bitter, what comes to mind whenever you think of the situation? But you can confess their sins all day long and not get your joy back.

Their sin comes to mind, and it covers up your sin that's separating you from God: your bitterness.

13. You might use vague terms to try jumping sideways along the cliff edge. "I think that, generally speaking, I have certainly sinned in *some* ways." Or you might say, "I never said I was perfect." Why do you not want to tell God the particular way in which you were imperfect this time?

Pride never wants to admit to specific wrongdoing. We think that pseudoconfessing allows us to keep a shred of self-respect (but of course, sin has taken that from us already).

14. In the space below, draw a triangle with an apex at the top. Put the word *God* there. If you are one of the other corners, what happens when you move along the line toward God, and somebody else on the other corner does the same?

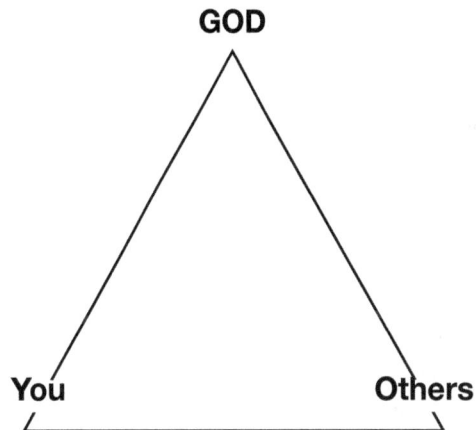

Both of you get will get closer to each other as you move toward God.

Answers for Lesson 4: Restitution—The Forgotten Duty

1. Look up Leviticus 6:1–7. In verse 1, who is speaking, and who is being spoken to?

The Lord himself is speaking to Moses.

2. In verse 2, when a man wrongs his neighbor in some kind of property transaction, who is he really sinning

against?

He's committing his crime against the Lord.

3. In verse 3, does it matter if a man finds something that belongs to someone else and lies about it afterwards?

Yes it does matter—he's sinning.

4. In the fourth verse, what is the basic duty that he has if he has done this sort of thing?

Basically, if you steal something in any way, you have to give it back.

5. In verse 5, when he restores what he has deceitfully gotten, what does he add to it?

He is to add a fifth of its value.

6. Once he has done this, what does he need to do in relation to the Lord, since it is the Lord he has sinned against?

He has to bring a sin offering to the Lord (which is a ram without blemish).

7. Look up Hebrews 10:1–4. Since Jesus has come and died on the cross, is there any need for us to offer a trespass offering?

No—the sin offering was a shadow of Jesus's sacrifice.

8. If a thief cannot pay the amount back, what do the Scriptures allow for (Exod. 22:3)?

The thief himself can be sold as a slave to pay for the entire theft.

9. We might say that we did not *mean* to harm our neighbor's goods. But does the Bible require restitution only if you meant it on purpose? What is required for culpable negligence (Exod. 22:5–6), not just for deliberate theft?

Even for culpable negligence, you must make full restitution, from the best of your own possessions.

10. We might say that "it broke" when I was borrowing it. What scriptural contingencies distinguish between borrowed and rented (Exod. 22:14)?

If the thing breaks when the owner isn't there, and you borrowed it, you have to pay to replace it. But, if you rented it (with money), the money you paid to rent it covers possible breakage.

11. We might say that we can't make restitution because it is simply impossible to do so. We can't remember who we stole it from, or we can't find them. If so, then where should the money go (Num. 5:5–8)? *We certainly don't get to keep it.*

The money should go to the priest.

12. Someone might say that the coming of Jesus has wiped the slate clean, and want this to mean that restitution is not necessary. But how would this apply to the situation Luke describes (Lk. 19:10)? Shouldn't this make restitution a joy?

Zacchaeus was so thankful to be saved by Jesus that he went above and beyond the requirements of the law. He was acting from the grace of a changed heart, and not just the requirement of the law against stealing.

13. Look up Ephesians 4:28, and summarize it in your own words.

[Answers may vary] We must stop stealing and instead work for a living, not just so we'll have money for ourselves, but so we'll have something to give to the poor.

Answers for Lesson 5: Assurance of Salvation

1. According to this passage (1 Jn. 5:13), why did John write to those who believe?

John wrote so that they would know they had eternal life, and so they'd believe on the name of Jesus.

2. If he wants them to know this, is it reasonable to assume that it is possible to know?

Yep.

3. Look up 1 John 3:14. If we love the brethren, what do we therefore know?

We know we have passed from death to life.

4. Not only is this love an evidence to ourselves that we are Christians, it is also an evidence to those around us that we are Christians. Look up what Jesus said in John 13:34–35. If the Christians love each other, what do all men recognize as a result?

They'll recognize that the Christians really are Jesus's disciples.

5. The second mark of a Christian can be seen in 1 John 2:3. We know that we have come to know God if we do something. What is that something?

If we keep God's commands, we know Him.

6. Look up Hebrews 12:7–8, and answer this question. When you endure chastening, what is happening?

God is proving that you're His child.

7. If someone is not chastened, then what does this make him?

It proves that that person is not a true child: they're illegitimate.

8. Read Hebrews 12:5–6. Chastening is a sign of what?

It's a sign of God's love and being received by Him.

9. The fourth mark of assurance can be found in 1 Corinthians 1:18. Look that passage up, and write down the difference shown between two kinds of people when the cross is preached.

Those who are saved see the power of God in the cross, but those who are dying in sins think the cross is foolishness.

10. The fifth mark has to do with the truth. Look up Romans 10:9. In that passage, someone will be saved if

they do two things. What are those two things?

Confess that Jesus is Lord, and believe in your heart that He was raised from the dead, and you'll be saved.

11. Look up John 5:24. If a man hears the words of Jesus, and believes on the Father who sent Him, what does he have?

He has everlasting life.

12. What will he not come into?

He won't come into judgment.

13. And why will that not happen?

He won't come into judgment because he has passed from death to life.

14. Look up 1 John 4:13. If God has given us His Spirit, then what two things do we know as a consequence?

We know we live in God, and God lives in us.

15. When the Spirit is given to a man, what does He make that man want to cry out?

He makes him want to cry out to God, "Father!"

16. And what would this seem to indicate?

If he wants to cry out "Father" to God, he has been born again into a new relationship with God, and God now is his Father.

17. So then, in summary, what are the six marks of a true Christian?

A true Christian is characterized by:

1. Love (of other Christians).
2. Obedience (to God's commands).
3. Being disciplined (God chastens His children).
4. Understanding spiritual things (starting with the gospel).
5. Confessing that Jesus is Lord (and believing the gospel in the heart).
6. Receiving the Spirit (so that he knows God is his Father).

Answers for Lesson 6: Resisting Temptation

1. According to this passage (1 Cor. 10:13), will God ever allow us to be locked up in temptation, with no way out except by sinning?

No—he has promised that temptations come paired with a way of escape in order to resist them.

2. Jesus instructs us to pray about temptation. Look up Matthew 6:13, and write down what He expects us to pray for there.

That God wouldn't lead us into temptation, but instead deliver us from the evil one.

3. What are we told to ask for in Hebrews 4:16?

We are told to ask for mercy and grace when we need it.

4. In Titus 2:11–12, what does Paul tell us about what the grace of God teaches?

God's grace teaches us that we need to live in a sober, righteous, and godly manner, refusing to give in to ungodliness and lusts.

5. Look up Proverbs 15:8. What does it say about the upright?

When the upright pray, it delights God.

6. And now look up Zephaniah 3:17. What does God rejoice over there?

He rejoices over us.

7. Look up Romans 6:12. What are Christians there told to not let happen?

We are told to be careful to make sure sin doesn't rule our bodies so that we have to obey our bodies' lusts.

8. Look up Hebrews 2:18. Who is tempted there?

Jesus Himself was tempted.

9. Now look up Hebrews 4:15. In how many ways was Jesus tempted?

Jesus was tempted in every way like we are.

10. Even though these built-in desires are not inherently sinful, they can be used, quite effectively, to draw us into sin. This is to be expected. The Bible gives Christians many repeated warnings about the lusts of the flesh. For just one example, look up 1 Peter 2:11. What wars against the soul?

Fleshly lusts war against our souls.

11. When we are tempted, we shouldn't blame God for it. Look up James 1:13–15. Who does not draw us into temptation? And what draws us away into temptation?

God doesn't draw anyone into temptation; we are enticed into temptations by our own desires.

12. Look up Nehemiah 4:17–18. What two instruments did each Israelite have?

They had construction materials in one hand (probably a trowel for masonry) and a weapon in the other.

13. The comparison is made in Proverbs 25:28. What is a man without self-control compared to?

He is like a city without walls (completely unprotected).

Answers for Lesson 7: Intelligent Bible Reading

1. Look up Deuteronomy 8:3. What is the basis of man's life? What is not?

The basis of a man's life is every word that God speaks, not food alone.

2. Suppose you are praying about whether to ask a girl to marry you. You pray and open your Bible at random to Jeremiah 16:1–2. What does God tell you there?

God apparently tells you not to get married or have any kids.

3. Why did Jesus say it is important to visit your

optometrist regularly (Mt. 6:22–23)?

If you have good eyes, then your body will be full of light!

4. Look up Acts 17:11, and answer the following question. What two things exhibited the nobility of the Berean Christians?

They received Paul's preaching with readiness, and then searched the Scriptures every day to make sure what he was saying was true.

5. Consider the importance of 1 Corinthians 4:6. What did Paul want the Corinthians to learn?

He wants the Corinthians not to form factions based on specific people or parties, but instead to base their opinions in "what is written"—the Bible.

6. Which party was the superfactional party in 1 Corinthians 1:12?

They were all being factional, but the superfactional group was the "of Christ" faction.

7. Like certain men of Issachar (1 Chr. 12:32), we should know how the Word applies to the current situation. What were they able to do?

The men of Issachar had an understanding of the times and could discern what Israel needed to do.

8. Look up 2 Peter 3:15–16. What do unstable people do to the Scriptures, and what is the result?

Unstable people twist the Scriptures, and they end up destroying themselves.

9. Look up Luke 1:2–4. How should we take what he wrote?

We should take it as the literal truth—Luke says he set out to write a factual, historical account, based on thorough research from eyewitnesses.

10. Look up Revelation 21:9–12. What indication of symbolism is there?

John uses striking images (clear light like a gem, etc.) and common themes from the rest of Scripture (lots of twelves, etc.) to show us the Christian church in a poetic way.

Answers for Lesson 8: Pleasant Words

1. So, look up Proverbs 16:21–24. In verse 21, who is known as prudent?

The wise in heart is prudent.

2. Notice the general flow in this passage, which is heart to mouth. What results from sweetness of the lips?

Sweet lips increase your learning.

3. Wisdom in the heart leads to sweetness on the lips, which in turn causes others to learn (v. 21). What, like wisdom, is also in the heart, and is described as a wellspring of life, bubbling up (v. 22)?

Understanding is a wellspring of life (if you have it).

4. But what bubbles up out of the heart of the fool?

Correction bubbles out of the heart of a fool.

5. What instructs the mouth of a wise man (v. 23)?

A wise man's heart tells his mouth what to say.

6. Moreover, what does his heart add to his lips, amounting to a reinforcement of the same thing (v. 23)?

His heart also adds learning to his lips.

7. Pleasant words are described as what, going down to the soul and down to the bones (v. 24)?

Pleasant words are like honey, sweet and healthful.

8. Look up Proverbs 15:28. What does the heart of the righteous do with regard to words?

The heart of the righteous studies how to answer well.

9. This is in contrast to the mouth of the wicked, which does what?

The mouth of a wicked man pours out evil.

10. What is the point of conversation in Ephesians 4:29?

Conversation is for edification—building up to impart grace.

11. In Proverbs 25:11–12, what is compared to jewelry in the right place?

A fitting word is like jewelry in the right place.

12. In Proverbs 10:32, what do the lips of the righteous know?

They know what is acceptable.

13. In Proverbs 15:23, what is so good about a good word?

You can find joy in giving it.

14. Notice that everywhere the Scriptures link the tongue and the heart. What is the nature of the interesting comparison in Proverbs 10:20?

The tongue of the righteous is compared to the heart of the wicked—and the righteous man's tongue is worth far more than the wicked man's heart.

15. In Proverbs 10:11, what is the mouth of a righteous man? But what covers the mouth of the wicked?

It's a well of life, but violence covers the wicked man's mouth.

16. And what is a wholesome tongue in Proverbs 15:4?

It's a tree of life.

Answers for Lesson 9: Difficult Differences

1. Look up Philippians 2:1–5. If there is any consolation in Christ (v. 1), and there is, and if God provides any comfort of love, and He does, and if He creates fellowship in the Spirit, which He certainly does, if there is a deep empathetic connection in the gut between

Christians, then what does he want them to do, right at the beginning of v. 2?

Christians should be like-minded.

2. How would we go about fulfilling Paul's joy? What is the first thing (v. 2)?

First, we can fulfill Paul's joy by being like-minded.

3. And the second?

Second, we can love the same thing.

4. The third?

Third, we can agree with each other.

5. And the fourth?

Lastly, we can have one mind with other Christians.

6. In verse 3, what should we guard ourselves against?

Be careful not to do things from selfish ambition or conceit.

7. What will lowliness of mind do for others?

It'll make sure we treat others as better than ourselves.

8. What should we esteem in the first place (v. 3)?

We should esteem other people.

9. What should we not think on first (v. 4)?

We shouldn't first consider our own interests.

Answers for Lesson 10: Strange Contentment

1. Let's start by looking up Philippians 4:6–7. According to this passage, what should make us anxious?

Nothing should be able to make us anxious.

2. As we avoid anxiety, how many things should we pray about?

We're to pray about every thing.

3. What should always be included in such prayer?

All our prayers should be made with thanksgiving.

4. As we make our requests to God, what will happen?

As we make requests, the peace of God will keep our hearts and minds, through Jesus.

5. Does this make sense to us?

No, it doesn't, because Paul says it surpasses all understanding (and that includes ours).

6. Now look up Colossians 3:15. What should rule in our hearts?

The peace of God should rule in our hearts.

7. What were we called to in one body?

We are called to let God's peace rule in our hearts.

8. And what should we be in addition?

We should also be thankful.

9. So what is the armor that protects us?

The peace of God must be our armor (we mustn't be struggling to protect God's peace).

Answers for Lesson 11: Living in the Will of God

1. Look up James 4:13–17. Who is James addressing?

He's addressing people talking all about the future of their impressive business plans.

2. What is the problem with their plans?

The problem is, we don't have a clue what the future will actually contain.

3. What is their life actually like?

Their life is actually like a shred of mist.

4. What should they say instead of what they have been saying?

They should qualify their plans with "If the Lord wills…"

5. What are they rejoicing in?

The people he was addressing were rejoicing in their boasting.

6. What is the problem with it?

The problem is, that kind of conceited rejoicing is evil.

7. How does James define sin here?

You are sinning when you know something good you ought to do, and don't do it.

8. How many things does God work out (Eph. 1:11)?

God works out all of them.

9. What does God's will include (Mt. 10:29)?

God's will includes the death of something as small as a sparrow.

10. Was the death of Jesus a tragic mistake (Acts 4:27–28)?

Absolutely not—God had gathered together all the might of the Jews and Gentiles to do what He had already determined to be done.

11. Look up 1 Thess. 4:1–3. What is described as the will of God there?

It's God's will that we don't fornicate.

12. Is it the kind of "will of God" that can be thwarted?

Yes—many Christians are guilty of fornication when they know better (maybe all, once you include Jesus's rebuke of mental lust as adultery).

Answers for Lesson 12: Christ Hidden in Your Calling

1. Look up Exodus 31:1–5. Who did the Lord call in this passage?

He called Bezaleel, a talented craftsman.

BASIC ANSWERS TO THE STUDY QUESTIONS

2. And what was he filled with?

Bezaleel was filled with the spirit of God..

3. What four things resulted?

Bezaleel received wisdom, understanding, knowledge, and workmanship.

4. What was he able to do?

He could work with metal, stone, wood, and anything else you might want.

5. What were we created for? What does Genesis 2:15 say?

We were created to tend the earth and protect it.

6. How many days should we work (Exod. 20:9–11)?

We should work for six days per week.

7. When we work, who should we remember is watching (Col. 3:23)?

We do our work like we were working for God Himself (because we are).

8. When we receive the fruit of any work done for us, who should we receive it as a gift from (Mt. 6:11)?

We should receive it as a gift from God: our daily bread.

Answers for Lesson 13: Desire Runs Deep

1. First, look up Matthew 20:1–16. At the end of this story, why did the workers murmur against their employer?

They complained that it wasn't fair for those who worked only an hour to get paid the same amount as those who worked the whole day.

2. What did he say in reply?

He said it was indeed fair—he paid them what they'd agreed to work for, and he could do what he wanted with his money as far as the latecomers were concerned.

3. What inversion sums the whole thing up?

The last will be first, and the first last.

4. Look up Genesis 2:9. Why would anybody want to eat the fruit that God made available?

The trees look really tasty and also really are good food.

Answers for Lesson 14: Heavier than Wet Sand

1. Look James 4:1–3. In a rhetorical question, in the first verse James wants to know the origins of what?

James wants to know where wars and fighting in his readers come from.

2. In the second verse, what does the intense desire of "lust" lead to?

Intense desire leads to killing.

3. Why is the request refused when we ask God for it?

God refuses to grant our request because we ask wrongly, to spend it on our desires.

4. Now read James 4:4–6. It is not possible to be friends with two things at the same time. What are those two things?

You can't be a friend of the world and a friend of God.

5. What does the Bible say about the spirit that dwells in us?

Our spirit intensely desires to envy others.

6. What does God give us in response to this tendency we have to veer off toward envy?

God gives us more grace to resist this tendency.

7. Who does God fight? Who does He help?

God resists the proud, but the humble get His grace.

8. Outside of Christ, envy is the natural condition of all mankind. Before we were converted, what were we like? Look up Titus 3:3, and write down what environment non-believers dwell in.

Non-believers are not just disobedient to God, they're also foolish and deceived, completely subservient to many different desires and pleasures. They exist in hatred, maliciously hating others, and at the same time envious of everything about those same people.

9. *That* is what we are like. Now look up Romans 1:29. Name three of envy's companions.

Envy keeps company with murder, fornication, and deceit (not to mention all the rest of its acquaintances in the verses before and after: disobedience towards parents, evil, malice, strife, coveting, gossip, God-hating, insolence, pride, boasting, inventing wickedness, foolishness, faithlessness, heartlessness, ruthlessness, and "all manner of unrighteousness").

Answers for Lesson 15: Competition

1. Look up Philippians 2:3–4. No action should have the following two characteristics. What are they?

It shouldn't be done from strife or for vainglory.

2. What does lowliness of mind do for others?

Lowliness of mind makes you esteem others better than yourself.

3. Each person should not look out for what?

Don't look out for your own interests.

4. Instead of this, what should each person look out for?

Look out for the interests of others.

5. If you are an accomplished pianist, and somebody else couldn't find middle C if you let them use both hands, does the first guy have to pretend that the second guy is a "better" pianist than he is? What does Paul mean here by better?

No—the musical illiterate isn't a better musician, but the skilled pianist needs to think that the illiterate is more important than he is.

6. Look up Proverbs 15:27. What does a greedy person do there?

A greedy person causes his family trouble.

7. Now look up 1 Timothy 3:3 and 3:8. What is the church required to do there?

The church is commanded never to elect elders or deacons who are greedy or covetous.

8. And should this issue be taken into account when we go to vote in civic elections (Exod. 18:21)?

Yep—Moses commands the Israelites to choose rulers who hate covetousness as one of their key attributes.

9. How do we know that the early Christians continued to hold property (Acts 5:4)?

We know the early Christians had private property because they were able to sell it for personal profit (and then give the profit to the church).

10. How do we know that they shared (Acts 4:32–33)?

Luke says the Christians did not claim anything for their own, but kept everything in common.

11. How many trees were prohibited in the Garden of Eden, and how many were allowed?

One was prohibited, and every other tree in the whole world was allowed.

Answers for Lesson 16: Real Ambition

1. Look up Luke 14:7–11. Why did Jesus tell this parable? What did He notice?

Jesus told this parable to guests, because he noticed that the guests all rushed to pick the place of honor at the table.

2. According to His teaching, what should we not do at a wedding?

We shouldn't take the place of honor.

3. Why shouldn't we do this?

Don't take the honored place, because someone more distinguished than you might have been invited, and then the host will kick you out of the best place to give it to the guest of honor (and maybe move you all the way to the lowest seat).

4. If that were to happen, what would be the effect on us?

We would be humiliated.

5. So what approach should we take to the seats of honor?

When you come, take the lowest place, and then you'll get moved up by the host.

6. Is the lesson here to never sit in a seat of honor? If not, what is the lesson?

The point of the lesson isn't to avoid seats of honor, because Jesus gives instructions on how to get a place of honor. The lesson is how to be humble and then be exalted in the right way.

7. What is the bottom-line principle that Jesus gives?

The principle is that those who exalt themselves will be humbled, but those who humble themselves will be exalted.

Answers for Lesson 17: The Meaning of Masculinity

1. Look up Genesis 1:26–28. This passage contains what is called the cultural mandate. What pattern does God use to make man?

God uses his own image as the pattern for man.

2. Man was to have dominion over what?

Man was to have dominion over the whole earth: fish, fowl, livestock, and all other animals.

3. After the list of creatures is given, over which man has dominion, what is he then told to do?

Man is told to be fruitful and increase in number, to fill up the earth and subdue it, and to rule over all of the creatures.

4. Now some might want to assume that this cultural mandate was negated by the fall of man into sin, but God repeats the mandate again after the flood. Look up that passage (Gen. 9:1). Are there any significant differences?

After the flood, the animals are given to men for food (instead of just the plants), and animals will fear mankind.

5. Look up Matthew 28:18–20. What are we told to do there?

We are told to teach the nations to do what Jesus commanded, and to baptize them in the name of the Father, Son, and Holy Ghost.

6. Look up Genesis 2:15. What did God give man to do?

God gave man the Garden of Eden to work and to take care of.

7. What was the promise that God gave us in Genesis 3:14–15?

God promised that men will crush the serpent's head.

8. The last aspect is that men are to be glory-bearers. Look up 1 Corinthians 11:7. What is man described as being there?

Not only is man the image of God, he's also the glory of God.

9. And what is woman described as being?

The woman is the man's glory.

10. Look up 1 Corinthians 11:3. What is the head of man there?

The head of every man is Jesus.

11. What is the head of woman?

The head of every woman is man.

12. Look up Ephesians 5:23–24. What is the relationship of husband to wife there?

The relationship is like that of Christ to the Church: Christ dies for the Church.

Answers for Lesson 18: The Meaning of Femininity

1. Now look up 1 Timothy 5:14. In this passage the apostle Paul is giving counsel to younger women on what they are to do. What should they become, with regard to the home?

They are supposed to be guides (or rulers or managers, depending on translation) of the home.

2. The phrase in the AV that is rendered "guide the house" is just one word in the Greek. That word is *oikodespotes*. The word *oiko* means "house." Does the rest of the word remind you of anything?

It looks like the word "despot"—a ruler who has absolute power.

3. From what is described here, does it appear that a woman has true authority in her home?

Yes—she is the home-ruler, and that means the authority in the home is hers.

4. Now look up Genesis 2:18–20. What did God say was "not good"?

It wasn't good for Adam to be alone.

5. What did God resolve to do about the problem?

He decided to make a helper for Adam.

6. After God said that He would create a helper suitable for Adam, what did He create first?

God created all the animals.

7. What did Adam do with all of them?

Adam named all the animals.

8. And what did he *not* find as he was naming the animals?

Adam did not find a helper.

9. And what is woman described as being?

She is described as suitable (or meet) for the man.

10. Look up 1 Corinthians 11:9. What does it say there?

The woman was created for the man (but not vice versa).

11. In Ephesians 1:22–23, how is the relationship between Christ and the Church described?

Christ is the head of the Church, and the Church is Christ's body and His fullness.

12. For the third aspect, look up Genesis 3:20. Why does Adam give his wife the name "Eve"?

Eve is named "Eve" because she was the mother of everybody.

13. In Genesis 4:1–2, who are the first two children born to Adam and Eve?

Their first two children were Cain and Abel.

14. In Deuteronomy 14:21, what is the requirement there?

The requirement is not to boil a baby goat in its mother's milk.

15. Why would this mean that women should not serve as combat troops?

Women shouldn't be soldiers because that would be turning someone meant to be a life-giver into a death-dealer (in violation of Deut. 14:21).

16. What is wisdom described as being in Proverbs 1:20?

Wisdom is a woman.

17. What does she do in Proverbs 9:1?

Lady Wisdom builds her house.

18. Look up 1 Corinthians 11:7. What does it say about woman in her relationship to man?

The woman is the glory of the man.

19. Now what does it say in Proverbs 12:4 about a virtuous woman's relationship to her husband?

She is a crown for her husband.

20. What do you do with a crown? Where do you wear it?

Since a crown is a symbol and a glory, you display it—on your head.

21. When you put it on your head, do you wrap it up in a burka?

No. That defeats the purpose.

Answers for Lesson 19: Relationships

1. Look up Colossians 3:18–21. First, what are wives told to do?

Wives must submit to their husbands.

2. What are husbands told to do?

Husbands must love their wives.

3. What are they told to *not* do?

They must not be bitter toward their wives.

4. Dependent children are told to do what?

Children must obey their parents.

5. In what areas?

Children must obey their parents in all things.

6. What does the Lord think of this?

Obedience to parents pleases God.

7. Look up James 4:1–3. What causes conflict?

Conflict comes from our desires.

8. And do people ever have such strong desires when it comes to members of the opposite sex? This is not a

trick question.

Yes, they do.

Answers for Lesson 20: Differences between Guys and Girls

1. Look up Ephesians 5:25–28. What are husbands told to do for their wives?

They are to love their wives.

2. This love is compared to what other kind of love?

A husband's love is like Christ's self-giving love for the Church.

3. What does Jesus do for the Church in v. 26?

Christ cleanses the Church.

4. What is the end result? What does the bride of Christ look like as a result of being loved in this way?

The result is that the Church is glorious: holy, without spots or wrinkles or stains or anything like that.

5. If a man loves his wife this way, then who does he also love?

If a man loves his wife like that, he also loves himself.

6. Look up Proverbs 14:12 and 16:25. There is a way that seems *what* unto a man?

There's a way that seems right to you.

7. But the end is what?

But that way ends in death.

8. Now look up Proverbs 5:3–5. Is the woman in v. 3 attractive?

Yes—kissing her is sweet like honey and smooth like oil.

9. So what is the nature of the caution?

In reality, she is as bitter and as sharp as anything you can imagine.

10. What should you consider?

She may look good, but she leads to hell.

11. In the space below, draw two vertical lines, side by side, with about three inches between them. This is what we might call the zone of vulnerability. All guys are on one side and all girls are on the other.

Guys   **(zone of vulnerability)**   **Girls**

12. Look up 1 Timothy 5:1–2. What does Paul tell Timothy to be very careful to do?

Paul tells Timothy to treat younger women as sisters with all purity.

13. Look up 1 Corinthians 11:9. Who was created for whom?

The woman was created for the man.

14. Now look a few verses down. In vv. 11–12, does this mean that men can be independent of women?

No, men aren't independent of women, because every man is born by a woman.

Answers for Lesson 21: Defining Cool

1. Look up 1 John 2:15–17. We are commanded to not love two things. What are they?

We are not to love the world or the things in the world.

2. If a man loves the world, what can we say about him?

John says we can know that the love of the Father isn't in that guy.

3. There are three things that are described as being "in the world." What are they?

The lust of the flesh, the lust of the eyes, and the pride of life are everything in the world.

4. Look up Genesis 3:6. What three things attracted Eve to the forbidden fruit?

The tree tasted good, looked good, and would make her wise.

5. Can you see any correlation between the passage in 1 John and this Genesis passage?

The fruit attracted Eve through the flesh (it tasted good), the eyes (it was pretty), and through pride (people "in the know" always seem to be cool)—in other words, the three lusts of the world were present (and deceitful) since the very beginning of mankind.

6. Back in 1 John 2:17, what passes away, and what abides forever?

Both the world and worldly desires are passing away, but a person doing the will of God abides forever.

7. Look up Leviticus 19:28. Two things are prohibited. What are they?

Scarring yourself for a dead relative or getting a tattoo is prohibited.

Answers for Lesson 22: Authenticity

1. Look up Matthew 23:5. When Jesus chastises the Pharisees here, what was their basic problem?

The basic problem of the Pharisees is that their main reason for doing anything was so people would see them and be impressed.

2. What did they do in order to be noticed by men?

They would put on extra-wide phylacteries and extra-large prayer shawls to be extra-religious.

[Note: a phylactery was something that Pharisees would tie onto their foreheads or hands, containing sentences from the law.]

3. Now are there different ways that this same problem could be exhibited, without using phylacteries or borders of garments at all? For example, like "my Bible is more underlined than yours"? Give your own example.

[Answers may vary] "My family sits closer to the front of the sanctuary than yours does," or "I wear a wooden cross necklace, have a Trinity symbol hanging from my rearview mirror, and have a fish on the back of my car."

Answers for Lesson 23: Handling Money

1. So first look up Matthew 6:19–24. What are we not supposed to do in the first instance?

We're not supposed to store up treasures on earth.

2. Why not?

Don't do that, because moths, rust, thieves, and all manner of things destroy or remove earthly treasure.

3. What are we to do rather instead?

Instead, we should store up treasure in heaven.

4. And what reason is given?

Store up treasure in heaven because it's safe there.

5. What follows your treasure?

Your heart ends up with your treasure, whether on heaven or earth.

6. What causes your whole body to be full of light or vice versa?

Having a good or bad eye causes that.

7. What does Jesus say is impossible?

It's impossible to serve two masters.

8. And what was God's competitor in this instance?

Money is God's competitor.

9. Look up 1 Corinthians 9:13–14. How were those who preached the gospel to live?

Preachers are supposed to make a living from preaching the gospel.

10. Look up 1 John 4:20. If we don't love our neighbor, what can we not say?

If we don't love our neighbor, we can't say we love God.

11. Look up Proverbs 11:25. What happens to a generous person?

A generous man will get lots of money.

12. What happens to him in Proverbs 22:9?

A generous man will get blessings.

13. And what is the final lot of the generous person in Isaiah 32:7–8?

A generous man will be able to stand because of his generous deeds.

14. What are we told to do in Proverbs 27:23?

Proverbs says to be diligent to know how your assets are doing.

15. Yes, you must provide, and please look up 1 Timothy 5:8. What is the condition of someone who doesn't provide?

If you don't provide for your family, you're worse than an unbeliever.

16. What does a good man do for his grandchildren (Prov. 13:22)?

He leaves an inheritance for them.

17. Look up 1 Timothy 6:17. Why does God give us wealth?

God gives us wealth so we can enjoy it.

18. Look up Deuteronomy 8:17-18. Why does God give us the power to get wealth?

God gives us that power to establish and confirm His covenant with us.

19. And why should we rejoice before God (Deut. 12:7)?

We should be glad because God has blessed us.

20. When God judged the Israelites, what was the judgment for (Deut. 28:47–48)?

The Israelites were judged because they didn't serve God with joyfulness, gladness of heart, and abundance in everything.

Answers for Lesson 24: Dealing with Fear

1. To begin our study of fear, look up Luke 12:4–7. Jesus commands us not to fear a particular group. Who are they?

Jesus says not to fear people who can kill you.

2. Why should we not fear them?

Don't be afraid of them, because they can't do anything after that.

3. Whom should we fear?

We should fear God.

4. Why?

Because God can kill you, and then throw you into hell.

5. What additional reason is given for not being fearful?

God doesn't forget even one sparrow, and we're worth lots of sparrows.

6. Look up 1 John 4:18. What does love do to fear?

Love casts out fear.

7. Why?

Love drives out fear, because fear is based on punishment, but perfect love is not.

8. For example, what is the beginning of knowledge (Prov. 1:7)?

Fear of the Lord is.

9. How did the witnesses of the empty tomb depart from there (Mt. 28:8)?

They were afraid but still filled with joy.

10. What rests upon those who fear the Lord (Lk. 1:50)?

God's mercy is on those who fear Him.

11. What three things went together when the people saw Jesus heal the paralytic (Lk. 5:26; cf. 7:16)?

Amazement, praise, and fear all went together.

12. What two things did the early church combine in their walk (Acts 9:31)?

The early church combined fear of the Lord and comfort in the Holy Spirit.

13. What does the fear of God enable us to perfect (2 Cor. 7:1)?

Fear of God helps with perfecting holiness (sanctification).

14. How are we to work out our salvation (Phil. 2:12–13)?

We are to work out our own salvation with fear and trembling.

15. How can we submit to one another (Eph. 5:21)?

We are able to submit to each other in the fear of God.

16. What should our worship of God be like (Heb. 12:28–29)?

Our worship should be reverent and fearful, for God is a fire.

Answers for Lesson 25: Sweet Sleep

1. Look up Proverbs 3:21–24. What should not depart from a young man's eyes?

A young man's eyes need wisdom and discretion.

2. What will be life to his soul, and grace to his neck?

Sound wisdom and discretion will be life and grace.

3. What will happen as he walks along the way?

He won't stumble; he'll walk safely.

4. What will not happen as he lies down?

He won't be afraid when he rests.

5. What will happen?

His sleep will be sweet.

6. Look up Psalm 127:1–2. What can a man not do by himself?

All of a man's labor is vain without God—he can't even sleep.

7. If God acts on his behalf, what will he receive?

He will receive sleep.

8. What happens if God lifts up the light of His countenance upon us (Ps. 4:6–8)?

We'll get gladness in our heart, and peace, and sleep in safety.

Answers for Lesson 26: In Summary

1. First, we want to make sure that our Christian life is God-centered. His glory is more important than our happiness, and the only basis for our true happiness is to know and acknowledge this. Look up Isaiah 6:1–8, and read through it carefully. If worship is presenting yourself to God for service, and not simply being awestruck at His glory, where does the worship in this passage occur? How is the idea of worship communicated?

The worship happens when Isaiah offers to be God's messenger (v. 8). Isaiah is struck with God's glory, cleansed, and then becomes God's servant.

2. Before God sends Isaiah out, He sends angels to cleanse his lips. This is important. Look up Hebrews 10:16–18. There are two main characteristics of the new covenant that are mentioned. What are they?

God has put His law on the hearts and minds of the people of the new covenant, and He has promised not to remember His people's sins any more.

3. What two things happen if we confess our sins to God (1 Jn. 1:8–10)?

Jesus forgives them and cleanses us from all unrighteousness.

4. Now look up Leviticus 6:1–7, and read it through carefully. Now in the fourth verse, what is the basic duty that a man has if he has done this sort of thing?

A man who has stolen in any way must give what he stole back.

5. According to 1 John 5:13, why did John write to those who believe?

John wrote so that they would have eternal life and believe on the name of the Son of God.

6. If he wants them to know this, is it reasonable to assume that it is possible to know?

Yes, that's the only way that makes sense.

7. According to 1 Corinthians 10:13, will God ever allow us to be locked up in temptation, with no way out except by sinning?

You never are forced to sin; God promises that there's always a way of escape.

8. Look up Deuteronomy 8:3. Why should we be committed to intelligent Bible reading? What is the basis of man's life? What is not?

We must read the Bible because the only basis for life is the words that proceed from God's mouth (not simple physical nourishment like bread).

9. What should be the point of our conversation (Eph. 4:29)?

Communication should be for the purpose of building the listeners up (edification).

10. Now let's look up Philippians 4:6–7. According to this passage, what should make us anxious?

We should not be anxious for anything.

11. When we work, who should we remember is watching (Col. 3:23)?

God is watching what we do.

12. Look up James 4:1–3. What does James want us to understand the origins of?

He wants us to understand the origin of the conflict among ourselves.

13. What does the Bible say about the spirit that dwells in us?

Our spirits veer toward envy.

14. Look up Luke 14:7–11. From that passage, explain why Jesus told this parable. What did He notice?

Jesus told this parable to give a lesson on honor and humiliation, because He noticed that guests always picked the places of honor.

15. According to His teaching, what should we not do at a wedding?

Jesus says not to sit in the seat of honor at a wedding.

16. So what approach should we take to the seats of honor?

We should sit in the least honorable seat, so the host will move us up to a better one.

17. Is the lesson here to never sit in a seat of honor? If not, what is the lesson?

No, because Jesus is describing the proper way to sit in a seat of honor. The lesson is that if you humble yourself you'll be exalted, but if you honor yourself you'll be humbled.

18. Look up 1 John 2:15–17. We are commanded to not love two things. What are they?

We are not to love the world or the stuff in the world.

19. There are three things that are described as being "in the world." What are they?

The lust of the flesh, the lust of the eyes, and the pride of life are what the world has.

20. Look up Genesis 3:6. What three things attracted Eve to the forbidden fruit?

Eve was attracted by the fruit's taste (flesh), its beauty (eyes), and its knowledge of good and evil (pride).

21. Look up Proverbs 11:25. What happens to a generous person?

A generous person is given lots of things himself.

22. Now turn to Luke 12:4–7. Jesus commands us not to fear a particular group. Who are they?

We shouldn't be afraid of killers.

23. Why should we not fear them?

We shouldn't fear them because all they can kill is the body.

24. Whom should we fear?

Instead, we should fear God, who can kill our bodies and then throw our souls into hell.

25. Look up Proverbs 3:21–24. What should not depart from a young man's eyes?

A young man must keep sight of wisdom and understanding.

26. What will not happen as he lies down?

He won't be afraid.

27. What will happen?

His sleep will be sweet.

28. In all these things, whom should we always trust?

God is the one who can always be trusted.